I0791132

ECCENTRIC ADULATIONS

"CRAZY LOVE"

JAMIL MAY

Archway Publishing books may be ordered through booksellers or by contacting:

Archway Publishing
1663 Liberty Drive
Bloomington, IN 47403
www.archwaypublishing.com
844-669-3957

ISBN: 978-1-6657-4164-4 (sc)
ISBN: 978-1-6657-4165-1 (e)

Library of Congress Control Number: 2023905941

Print information available on the last page.

Archway Publishing rev. date: 02/01/2024

DEDICATION

This goes out to all the women I've ever loved. Whether it was correctly or incorrectly my heart needed to heal and learn to love itself. I pray yours does the same.

PREFACE

Most of the people I know have already troubled me with questions as to why I am writing a book about love. What do I know that hasn't been told already? What could I spend fifteen chapters consulting about? Well for starters, experience is the one thing that I am discussing. Since the beginning of time; love has been in our faces with our loving parents or guardians. Then trickling down into our immediate to extensive families, but does love begin and end there? Does love have a limitation? Should you only love your blood relatives unconditionally? These minor questions are what opened the vastness that Eccentric Adulations embodies. What is love?

I couldn't fathom the idea of love at first. I felt so stuck on the unhealthy ways that I felt. I grew accustomed to the toxic teachings of the generations before me. The "woe is me" mentality that never looked surreal. I always felt that those kinds of thoughts couldn't be considerate of someone else, which led me to a major stage in my life. The stage that is considered owning your faults and wrongs. *"Accountability."* When I hold myself accountable is when I truly notice the collateral beauty that love holds. When I held myself accountable, I realized the importance of my identity. As a person involved with another person it's important to remember your role. No matter what position you hold in someone's life it's personally on you to uphold your end of the bargain. I noticed often that when it comes to love, people drop the ball. Mistakenly loving with fear of losing, which in reality creates the loss. Which led me back to the initial question at hand. What's love? Is love a feeling? All I could utilize at the time; was the relationships I knew and that's what made me call love, crazy. After careful consideration I couldn't comprehend why I felt so many ways when considering all that I love.

As an adolescent you don't differentiate between love or infatuation; you know they both feel good. As you mature though not only do you look towards your parents/guardian but the media, the television, the movies, even our peers. These various pressures help us see what the idea of love truly means. Most people stop there and fantasize. Pondering on prince charming fairytales and films with successful conclusions. The idea of love must always be this feel-good entity that absorbs negative energy. When you become an adult, and have a fair share amount of relationships, you learn the harsh realities that love comes with. Those sleepless nights hoping they answer a call. Those raged fights that ended with forgiveness in your hearts. What about those in-depth conversations that took natural releases? Those kinds of situations lead directly to love just as the scene where he kissed her in the rain. We learn over time that love has various lenses and the one we look through is how we notice what love is. Maturing in love means learning what love is, but a mature person in love knows exactly what it takes to unconditionally love.

That's what triggered me at nineteen years old, maturing in love; seeking its truth. Love for me didn't start beautifully. Since I was a child, really every girl I happen to like never liked me back. I took that kind of stuff on the chin until I met someone, I thought I could love "forever." I spent a good nine to ten years learning what forever truly meant, not just to myself but those I chose to love. It took a decade to comprehend the various extremities that come with love. Once I experienced enough at home and in the world when it came to love, I evolved my train of thought. I considered religion for love. I considered unborn children for love. I considered myself for love. These minor considerations made me think deeper. How does God want us to love? What does a respectful man look like for my daughter? What does a responsible husband look like in his marriage? I couldn't find answers to most of my questions; so, I had to seek the answers within my life to draw some conclusions. This began as a search for love and ended up being a tale to tell many how to identify and healthily continue to love. I speak darkly throughout this story overshadowing the true beauty with the toxic energy we all seem to enjoy so much, including myself. The trauma written out is a culmination of a heart full of love and a mind full of rage. The story is called "Eccentric Adulations" which dismantles the idea of this crazy love we all seemingly can't live without. A love that would not manifest as beautifully if it didn't begin and end with self. Welcome to the craziest love that stems from the internal and affects everything externally.

INTRODUCTION

The love that most people enjoy today is either portrayed or presented. Whereas, unconditional love; is worked on continuously. Here lies an open dialogue between two figurative heads and one whole heart. Metaphorically, those heads fuel your heart's desires which then becomes the ultimate sacrifice. Eccentric Adulations is like a survival guide to the countless issues someone could face when dealing with love. "Love" is considered crazy for numerous reasons but the main one is because it will make you stay even when you know you should leave.

Love is crazy because you could be so frustrated in the moment and still be madly in love with a person. As a human you can fault yourself for your mistakes, but it doesn't mean you no longer love you. These are emotions and they sway from time to time and change your decisions. This makes love crazy because once its felt, you run into all these emotions. Love is a cycle but it's a journey that you are supposed to venture through with a significant other. When you venture through love with yourself you begin to organize your life. Loving yourself means forgiving yourself, doing for yourself, being present with yourself. Loving someone else isn't as important as loving yourself. You will notice that throughout the story.

This book is set up to connect to the world that surrounds me. This generation does not respect love. The world these days enjoy sex over love. Most people tend to fear falling in love because of the hurt or the need for someone else. My generation respectfully sucks at communicating for the purpose of understanding. The generation I come from are adult children begging to be heard. This makes the dating scene hard to trust these days. People do not fight fair anymore. The emotions run high, and the love becomes a loss. People nowadays tend to guard their hearts vigorously. There's no growth or God and as a result this lost generation forgot what makes love so beautiful. Society forgot how important date night, or sensual touch meant to lovers. This dissertation respectfully reminds the world of how dark love can become. The harsh realities of such a beautiful drug.

"Love" will make you stay just as much as it makes you leave, therefore; loving yourself becomes the most important thing. I didn't write this to vent about all the sadness love left me with. Hysterically there will be those who misunderstand the weight that love carries. Therefore, ignorantly they will miss the true story hidden within the elements. Love is just as dark as it is light and when it's cherished that same love will last until your next lifetime, still admiring that crazy ass love.

CONTENTS

FUCK LOVE

F*uck Love!?* Love is not ordinary nor is it extraordinary. I hate the feeling love brings to me. Love is so awful I wouldn't consider it a feeling. Love is a drug. The type of drug you can become addicted to. Love is such an invigorating drug that the very first high could last you over ten thousand lifetimes. Love feels so good while you're in it; that even the short romances are just as hard to let go of. The potion of love creates a dependency to be loved in a sense by anyone. As a result, the addiction leaves us all feening no matter how damaging it may be for the individual. *Why?* People are hopeless romantics; wishing one day they'll find the same love from the television. A love that is unachievable. The fiction that surrounds social media is the exhausted efforts, that aren't normally explained. *Love becomes a cycle.* An ongoing chase between two lovers in support of a never-ending theory, a theory that love can be admired in the afterlife if it's cherished. With or without interest, when love doesn't fuel you, sex will. Knowing that love is hard to find will turn any soul away from emotional romance. It can be exhausting trying to find harmony with another soul. Our world revolves around reproductive intimacy. Therefore, love becomes unobtainable to those who will not chase it. Honestly, you could lose who you are for love. Time will slip by and leave you wishing the love you started with can become the love that you are dealing with. Instead, give time to revitalizing the love that's shared because it's still the same love. Take your time with love. Here is a comparison, love is like crack. Within that first high, you are floating. Thereafter; you spend forever trying to recreate that feeling. That's love. More than usual when dealing with love you experience heartbreak. Heartbreak is the leading cause of depression. Those pieces of love lost could never return simply because of how broken we're all left. **FUCK LOVE!** How could there be hope for love when you can find older couples resenting the marriage they admired for decades? Not only old couples, but the general population also; divorce rates are higher than marriage rates. People tend to fall out of love and forget what they loved in their spouses to begin with. Nobody appreciates love anymore. Even still, there are countless questions we could all ask ourselves to pertain to love. What are the consistencies of love? What is love? How do you know you're in or out of love? Those are examples of valid questions when dealing with love. <u>*DISCLOSURE*</u> **LOVE KILLS! Somedays love leaves you face down in sorrow, sadness, even doubt.** Love will leave you dissecting yourself. There's no point for love when you could still be hurt in the end. No one knows the best way to maneuver through love because there are endless questions and unsaid things about love. That doesn't mean stop seeking knowledge about love. There are so many people that tell different stories but don't fail to remember your own experiences to recognize love. There's a lesson in everything that pertains to love, you must seek it. When observing love, take the time to understand that we each have two heads and one heart. The head we choose, will fuel our hearts desire.

Love won't always be a painful feat nor an inspiring feeling; but it's bittersweet to the taste. Some moments you wish ended quickly, while others you'd rather bask in for millenniums. Love can be viewed on an infinite spectrum. Love stands as the most complicated topic to discuss. If you have minimal understanding of what love is, it's a **choice.** Generally, the people who decide to experience love as a feeling end up hurt by love. "*Real love hurts!*" In the mist of pain, keep choosing love.

No matter what! Love must become the focal point in your existence. Whether its self-love or the love you have for someone else. Choose love. Then remember, despite the lows; neither gender nor preference decides who you love or who loves you back. There is someone on this planet for everyone to love. As a matter of fact, there's two humans for every person just based on population. This all depends on which head fuels your hearts desires. Normal human beings fear love and selfishly choose themselves over giving love a try. No matter what anyone says about love it's still the leading factor in success. Whether it's self-love or a spouse, love inspires even the darkest soul to reach its fullest potential. Love requires the best you must give no matter how much you'd rather remain stingy. When love fails, question yourself, what did I choose, because love is codependent on you. No matter the route you take love makes you analyze what's right or what's wrong in your life. Which includes your decisions. Nowhere in love will a wrong become right without the proper steps taken towards love. *Therefore, love requires sacrifice; but it's worth it.*

Love requires you to lose some people that may have been around for more than a lifetime. Love takes diligence but requires a lot of patience. Love takes putting your pride aside. Love takes away from the things you like. Love forces you to understand the feelings and thoughts of your significant other. This is where love becomes complicated. When you're in love you must put that person first. In other words, they matter before you matter because you trust they'll put you before themselves as well. Love is a mutual understanding. In love the rule is simply give and take. A cycle of one giving their all and one taking your all. It's continuous which is why in love you become dependent on your lover. In love you tend to always need each other. When it comes to love there will forever be those that finesse love which results to hurt. Those acts aren't considered love. Remember that love will always be the toughest pill to swallow. Love is still the most complicated topic to dissect because it is not simple to accept. Learn to trust love. Allow love to play its role in your relationship without thinking the worst. Even when the time arises when you all are hurting one another intentionally. Relax the two-way streets of pain and learn from the mistakes we all tend to make. In life we get caught up and we tend to forget about the person we love. I think it's time we realized love for what it is. A simple yet continuous choice.

When it comes to love, be sure to ask yourself endless questions. The more you question love, the more you learn about what it may be for you as an individual. What are the things you love? What do you love about someone else? How are you attracted to the person you love? Love and infatuation are the two easiest things to confuse. When you are infatuated, you tend to think very shallow of the person. Looks. Voice. Body type. These things don't equate to a long-lasting relationship. Being honest with ourselves we don't want anyone that doesn't meet our visual standards, but we also can't marry beauty. Meaning we won't marry the best looking but low self-esteem person who has no internal value. We want to marry someone who's compatible with our heart's desires. We want someone we can't keep our minds off. Think meritoriously when you think of your lover. If you find yourself in betwixt the midst of love and infatuation not leaning to either side maybe, it's time to ask yourself another question. **Are you in love?** If you find yourself thinking both ways; that's considered using the two heads you were born with, as well as your heart. Even though we all have more than one mind to think with we only have one heart to please. The failure comes along when we give the most power to one mind. All genders fall short when they prefer thinking with their sexual reproductive organ. The wrong comes into play when you know you're intentionally hurting yourself as well as others. There's no love on that path. We all want the best looking with amazing features. We want someone with everything and more; but you must ask yourself, what does your heart desire? When it comes to your heart's desires you need both heads not just one. Only sex makes the heart colder and only using love turns your passions weaker. No matter what you choose as your desire, your heart will always tell you the truth. That's why intimacy is so vital in the relationship. Intimacy is considered a way to intertwine your soul with your loved one. Therefore, be sure to figure out your hearts desires as well as your significant others. Following love requires both partners' hearts and minds to connect as one, while sex becomes the addition. Emotional intimacy defines a relationship unity, therefore; loose screws leave room for individuality. Don't just screw them; choose them. According to the person ask yourself which mind should you use? How could you fuel your hearts desires? Is this love or infatuation?

I JUST WANT TO FUCK

JUST WANNA FUCK! I don't have time for love, I only wanted to see how vulnerable you'd become. Words get thrown like knives with no intent but to fuel our own egotistical tendencies. Frequently we hurt those that have different intentions than our own. That brings fear into relationships; knowing that you could love someone, but they like you for what you are offering. When you are infatuated, there isn't any applause for who you are or who you can be. There's only a lustful desire. Arguably we all know what love is. But love stems from the youngest most confusing times. It begins so early that we neglect its beauty once love hurts. We were told that love shouldn't hurt, which has broken up countless relationships. Love tends to be easier to accept when pain isn't involved. Selfishly we can only think of ourselves when it comes to love. Sex though? That simply becomes the narrow pathway between love and pain. Some of the most beautiful souls have become stripped of their innocence for a moment of pleasure. The fact that we use one another causes this worldwide war zone.

On the journey to finding love the only code society lives by is play or be played. Who has time for love when you're bound to get played regardless? Melancholically, I learned to play them before they played me. Staying ahead of the game keeps you ahead of the hurt. There is no such thing as love. *Fuck trust.* No matter who you are, if you're human;

pain is bound to catch up to you one day. Amidst hurt, most people fall in love but in the end the pain ruins even the loveliest marriages. Meaning, without preparation; love can and will hurt you. Choose love over infatuation. Out of those that are infatuated, most forget the hurt love causes. Besides, who wants to remember pain that's coming no matter what precautions are taken?

Loving someone for a moment's notice is an extremely painful plight. Whereas sex over love is like life without emotions, unenthusiastic. I've watched floods of women chase one guy that has an emotional coil full of hearts, only because they wanted his love. As a society we wholeheartedly want sex over love. Sadly, sometimes; sex only comes when you string people along. **SEX.** That's one of the biggest downfalls in the dating scene. As men we rather ejaculate than recognize the true beauty of someone else. Face it, that's the reality of things. Why go out on a date when there are countless women throwing themselves at me? For the guys reading, take time to understand the hurt you've faced in life. Heal. Then find a woman worth settling down for. Be a man your daughter would cherish even if you don't have one. As a man your decision making should mimic the same decisions you wouldn't mind your children making. Otherwise, you're doing it wrong. Thinking with your penis will lead you towards various trails of tears, especially for your victims. As for everyone, we fall short because we're human. Arguably, the person you are with doesn't sexually please you. Teach them. Maybe you'd rather have multiple partners. Let's not forget everyone doesn't keep themselves disease free. More than 1 million STI's are acquired daily. **DAILY!** We all have one heart to please, but we waste it on sexual pleasures. Having multiple partners, you lay in bed with will not help you find the right partner for holy matrimony. Don't get me wrong we all know sex feels amazing, especially when there are nothing tying the two of you together. In the end, you cannot control your heart. There could still be feelings. Don't try to ignore them just because you agreed to no ties. Your heart deserves love. It yearns for love. Without love we perish alone. As a society we're against love because it's more complex than sex. Love is the ultimate sacrifice for human beings. Giving up your body for the desire of sex could create yet another human being. Passion is magnificent. Sex is considered precious. No matter how rough it seems in porn; sex is an act for desire, which makes it intimate. Nevertheless, we ignore all these concepts because of pain. Pain from love derives from various people portraying a false sense of security for those that are vulnerable. Sex is so fulfilling until you've reached your climax. What happens when you hurt someone? How would you respond to them saying?

"My ignorance was innocence, stroked by your egotistical arrogance. I was stupid to think our hearts could beat as one. This was never love; I was only another trophy added to your collection."

How would you feel if that was something your daughter said to a man? She was in love while he just wanted to fuck. The addictions are the only things that need recovery. Those few moments of sexual pleasures ruined yet another soul. Being in love is scary because you must trust that they're in love with you too. How could anyone trust a love that cuts this deep?

Without judgement I understand all aspects of love affairs. I am still a man, so I thought with my dick as well. From experience I've played women and there were some women that played me. At some point you stop caring about love and there becomes a desire to fuck and add bodies to the figurative collection. Which in my opinion is deeply rooted? Either way I know, broken-hearted depression is real. Over time I learned to separate my head and heart because of broken-hearted depression. To all the girls I ever loved, I sincerely apologize for my insensitive actions. Being a man requires a journey through life alone. That journey can make any man resent anything. No matter how damaging life could've been it doesn't make breaking hearts okay. Experiencing heartbreak at a young age is detrimental for anyone. **LOVE KNOWS NO AGE. LOVE HAS NO BOUNDARIES. LOVE FEELS NO PAIN,** *only the person does.*

Broken-hearted depression is real in a sense that you never know when or how it could happen. I'll give you a personal yet real example of the reality that surrounds us all pertaining to love. Imagine your child at a gathering with friends, family, and their spouse. Of course, you are not in attendance. Between the ripe ages of ten and fifteen we were all inexpertly experienced. Imagine them in a dark corner of the room tonguing and touching, enjoying their sublime secrecy. This precious yet innocent fun made them feel confident. As if there wasn't anything more enticing than the peaceful lust of love. As time progress they separate but soon are surprised, that in an hour they missed each other. When they did see each other again that same secrecy was being shared with someone new. Come on. Think about it! Imagine this being you at that age. Being so young thinking you're in love. Assuming you knew one another. Especially if you've been on the same page for years no matter how young they were. They felt the true beauty of what love could be. That person knew everything. There were shared secrets. Private moments with possible tears. That young vulnerability meant love. Imagine your child having their heart ripped out and mutilated by love and as a parent you knew nothing about it. They spent awkward and embarrassing moments together. Loved every second of the time spent around one another. Then all those moments flash before their eyes when they see them touching and tonguing someone else. Imagine the pain they shared with each other. They were best friends to each other. The hurt nobody else knew, they told them. In their minds they had nothing or nobody but them. **IMAGINE THIS!** It felt like they were soulmates for each other. Undoubtedly, that very moment changed them forever. Imagine the separation this causes between you and your child. All because of those unspoken things. Imagine the decline your child could face alone from that situation. That's the moment you are losing them. Those issues they couldn't trust you with, those uncomfortable topics leave you constantly questioning your child. Remember they aren't interested in childlike things anymore. Their mind wonders to adult ventures. How could you save them from this?

How can you inform them about something you know nothing about? As a parent of course, you sense they're off, but you can't understand the emotions bared. From that moment forward, the child that lit up the night sky, now carries the weight of heartbroken depression. No matter what's presented in front of them they can't heal that traumatic moment. It's a scar and those things are stuck with you for the rest of your life. An emotional scar embedded deep in the heart. Now every decision they make comes right back to that lesson learned from the very first scar. Heartbreak, drunken down with misery can change someone. The road can lead anywhere. Drug abuse. Suicidal thoughts. Rebellion. Revolutions. Disobedience. Heartbroken depression can turn a beautiful world, dark in a matter of a few birthdays. Just a couple summer vacations ago your baby was full of joy; now they mope with sorrow. Take the time to realize the detriment that broken-hearted depression has on every soul no matter the age. Despite the boundaries that are set. Accepting every feeling of pain felt. Broken hearted depression is as real as it gets.

Despite what most of us think, people don't fall into mentalities that are emotionally damaging. Nobody wakes up and say, I'm so devastated, *FUCK LOVE!* Sex has always been easier than love. It's easier to find someone who admires sex over naturally falling in love. As a society we don't see a point in allowing ourselves to feel love. Love should be cherished like the rarest piece of art, while sex becomes the masterpiece. Sexual intercourse is arguably the best way anyone could feel. Sex is an art with two bodies. Filling one another's emptiness with passion is as beautiful as the Mona Lisa. Sooner than later, you learn people love you momentarily. Love is only there because there's something you offered them. The world is full of young-minded men and women loving people for the visuals portrayed not their true character.

What is the first thing you see when you notice a new man or woman walking past you? What if their eyes were always the first noticeable thing? Noticing one another soul for mere seconds then go back to living would be so divine. How memorable would first impressions be if eye contact was the most important thing? Arguably, that's not the world. We all tend to fill our hearts with various negative thoughts and or actions. It's a cataclysmic world out there and the more you pay attention, the more you'll see; the players, the played, and those who have no sorrow for other's feelings. Protect your heart until you sincerely know; this is love. Be patient. Love comes in many formal and informal appearances. Learn to move yourself. Love what you can do and who you are first. Find yourself in consideration with your hearts authentic understanding of yourself. Then true love will find you.

I THINK I'M IN LOVE WITH YOU

I THINK I'M IN LOVE WITH YOU! Do you really mean it? Could my love be that infectious? Love can be amazing if it's treated. For love to grow you must water it like a flower. Keep choosing to love but also keep showing loved ones that you care. Love is the only connection that brings two people together as one: in any manner. In essence, there could be a strong mental connection which stands most firm; that's love. There could be an excellent connection spiritually where you motivate one another; that's love. An emotional acceptance could keep love in balance as well; don't ignore any aspect of the love that can be shared. Love is what all heart's desire. It's easy to consider love as a feeling or an act of passion but when you progress in love you notice its identity. Love is as much of a **commonality** as it is an *understanding*. There must always be a neutral territory.

The only way to tell you're in love; will be time. Without specification, the only way to tell if your partner is in love with you is when or if they sacrifice for someone other than themselves. *LOVE REQUIRES SACRIFICE.* I cannot stress that enough. Being in love requires you to change your ordinary habits. When you are in love you will require; desire and aspire more out of that person for affectionate reasons. Be mindful of *expecting* things. Love yourself enough to meet your own expectations. Therefore, again; pack patience. Love is far from easy, especially when you have resentment towards it. Love is insensitive when it's real. Love challenges you. Loves likes to test you for every mental and emotional predicament. Love inspects your determination for the relationship to reach endless honeymoon phases. The test is complete when you are willing to make another more important than your own. Could you reach an existential ecstasy with someone?

How much can one truly love another? *Love is infinite.* **LOVE KNOWS NO BOUNDARIES.** It's irresponsible to place limitations on the amount you love someone. Love outpours from the body onto those connect to you. Love is breathtaking. Even if it's for a little while; love is enduring. Love is peculiar because pure sensitivity can be anger as well. Which makes love miraculous because you'll still stay.

Who wants to be seventy and alone? Loneliness seems peaceful at first but it's never in the cards for life. Our hearts yearn for love. We are rather selfish, choosing loneliness over selfless love because of its difficulty. Therefore, if it were any easier how could it still be love? The enjoyment a commitment brings drains the loneliness out of life. An existence is better with love. A heart connects directly to your soul and your soul feeds your hearts desires. A vivid picture of two heads and one heart would be your brain connecting to neurons which connects to your spirit. Thinking things through leaving no room for sentimental value will only fuel one head, *one-track mindedness.* Sexual pleasures are not a means of understanding a sympathetic attraction; those actions only fuel one head, *one-track mindedness.* Too much emotion causes an estrangement, which begins to fuel one head, *one-track mindedness._*Love is much more than a one-way street. Love is more complicated than our genetic make-up even though we have 86 billion neurons connect to our brains. One must have of balance of power and in balance, love will be found. No matter the time or place you will soon rely on one another. Here's a poem written to love…

"I forgot my sun and ignored my moon because you are the illuminating frequency that starts my night and ends my dreams. Love feels more than we do. Love fills me enough to trust my codependent need for you. It's because of love that I can say; I think I'm in love with you."

I often find us as humans losing love for humanity. We frown upon the ones around us expecting more from love. There's an expectancy for greatness to grow from their stagnant being. It's sad. How can you grow correctly without the right nutrients? In love you must be able to depend on them when all your chips are down. If your peace of mind involves love, you must respect your loved one. Humans are selfish by feeling we've done enough. When dealing with love pack a lot of patience because you'll need it. Trusting a relationship means allowing the growth process all the time it needs. Your hearts desires will fuel your entire being. When you use the words; I think I'm in love with you, I use it more than literally. I can eat, sleep, and breathe the very thought of your love. When it comes to love it can turn an impure heart admirable. The moment you feel sensitivity it begins to migrate into deeply rooted emotions. *Becoming rich with love.* Vulnerability was an understatement for the love that surrounded me. Thoughts can be arranged from impure: erratic, misguided, and or even impulsive. Love tends to confuse your mind. I'm connected through love. Love creates matches made from the heavens. Therefore, purity becomes intimacy.

Sex has never been better than love; but it's a damn good place to start. Love will always be the priority, but sex will forever be the emphasis in making love. When discussing intimate love, it's a lot better to be direct. Therefore, love drives me crazy, but sex brings me peace. In our softest moments, vulnerability never hides. Erections are sought out by moist fortifications. My mouth becomes a tool for you. Therefore, the aftertaste that lies between my lips embodies your delicateness. The silence of words that are coherent through exasperated breaths proves the need for this love. In those moments we're breathing the same air, my eyes keep our intimacy confined.

Although no words have been spoken; the tricks your tongue does fulfills all my passions. The excitement that overwhelms me brings us in harmony. Which turns our pretty secret into a seismic oceanic surf. Spontaneously, my paintbrush strokes can easily produce a work of art. This motion creates a need to be closer; meanwhile, we're already in unison. As I slowly assure you that you are mine, the exasperation becomes a delicate cry. While I penetrate the deepest parts of you there's only one thing left to do:

"Don't leave me because I'm in need of your love. I must have you in every sense pleasurable. I want to ease your mind, aesthetically. I want to fulfill your hearts desires, arrogantly. I crave your spirit and all its splendor. I love to be inside you routinely. I can't stand being away from you. Anytime you call my name just know I'm coming. In moments like this one I can honestly say I think I'm in love with you."

Reluctantly, my love for you is executed with exceptional interpretation. It is hard to believe your heart is in my hands but believe me with everything that I do, I always think of you. As I hold you through the night, I think of a million more ways to shower you with love. I think of the trauma you once faced, and it gives me a sense of urgency to protect you from any harm. I think I'm in love with you. Although our relationship has its many trials and tribulations my heart will forever remain complacent beside yours. I'm afraid of this feeling because nothing ever good came from me saying I think I'm in love with you. I've reached my lowest points in love trying to make it work. All the time it took to recover; I never thought at the end of the road I'd be blessed with you. I'll say it with pride; I know I'm in love with you. I'd make any sacrifice necessary to be able to be with you forever. If we're being frank, I'm afraid because I know I love you which means I'll always need you.

I NEED YOU

need you because emotions tend to be one of the hardest things to stand behind; yet and still love is such a beautiful emotion. With the right vibe love can be astoundingly sensual. Love would feel like the heavens stood upon the earth and decided to stare back at you. I found love in so many things. I could make a list, but that would be too many stories to tell. Passion ignites emotions in a way that you can't live without. Love is only as crazy of a matter because of passion. Passion fuels love by feeding desire. Have you ever stared into the night sky and accidentally spotted a shooting star? That's how fascinating love feels. Once you see the star, you feel special; you had a chance to wish upon it in hopes it comes true. Love is so unbelievable that even if it doesn't come true the hope was worthwhile. Amazingly you had a once in a lifetime experience by seeing a shooting star. Love to me is passionate. It's lucrative because it connects everything and everyone, from having self-love, to a love for your craft; love is interchangeably passionate. Call me biased but love is extraordinarily beautiful.

Most things should be infinite as far as love goes. Love should be so amazing that you learn how to pour your all into it. Learn the dynamics of love, therefore; once problems occur you know they're finite on the spectrum of love. Most things matter but the things we love show us what we're passionate about. Even the most minor thoughts on love could mean the world to us. Love makes everything complicated. Allow me to speak to her, in other words this would make more sense:

I need you baby. I love you more than the moon adores the sky. I seek your vastness daily; so, when I close my eyes, I think of your every desire. I listen to all your needs. You need to be held; secured. I would like to accommodate all your requests. Even though that may not be easy I think you're worth every effort that takes. I can be a bit selfish when I say I want all of you, so forgive me ahead of time. I hear all the songs your heart cries. You're so stunning because every song soothes my mind. I love you more than you'd ever know. I can assure you daily that you're so beautiful. I left no room for insecurities because they don't belong here between us. As crazy as that may seem trust that your heart is safe with me. I can provide you with loyalty so love can grow as you feel that sense of loyalty. I don't just want you; I need you in my life. Even if the time comes that we hurt each other, it's okay, because you're all I need most nights. I'll support you through anything. You're lovelier than caramel on a vanilla sundae. As wonderful as you are, I believe that God patiently made you, because you complete me. You're deserving of everything which includes devotion. I hope you feel the same. My heart flutters to Neptune just to align with the stars that are you. Even space with its endless light years has bounds compared to the unconditional love I promise to give you. I would take the time to build a ship with you and sail across the seas. For pure unity our efforts must remain consistent. As I built with you, the time spent to get to know you would be a dream come true. I wanted you to know that my heart has been producing beats that orchestrate ballads of adulations. I think it's beautiful that we have the time to build a solid foundation for our relationship. I love you, not metaphorically but emotionally. I love you more than the best eyes can see; the brightest mind could understand, or even the wisest man could comprehend. My love for you is immeasurable by man it's truly extraordinary.

I need you. I really need you, but there are far too many reasons for a single explanation. My need for you expands further than my own ordinary considerations. The dangers that come with loving you are the risks I am willing to take. I can't recall feeling before now, is this bliss? Inform me, what mystical powers does your aura carry; because I am involved? How will I know if this love has real meaning? I wouldn't mind expressing my emotions because I hide within my vulnerability. I need you because I can't come to peace with the fact that I'm weak for you. I want to cherish you until the end of the time. We can begin at a slow and steady pace; I have patience for you. Let's travel to another galaxy. No matter if it takes 2.5 billion light-years; my soul will forever cherish each moment. Although I'm afraid; I need you to know where my vulnerability hides because it's forever yours to keep. I need you just as much if not more than you need me. The old baggage I carry will be released for your love. If our efforts are equal, I don't mind making any sacrifice because I need you.

I need you because I've been injured. I'm an emotionless man seeking out the likes of you. Unfortunately, I haven't felt love long enough to know if I'm worth your time. Even with all my weaknesses, I will love you unconditionally. My words will become proven facts because it's up close and personal. Somedays I can't help but to love you gently. I am your King. Have faith in me because I will stand on the highest mountain and proclaim what your love means to me. Even when those days come where we say things we don't really mean, I already forgive you. I'll enjoy being able to whisper euphoric sentiments in a way that'll ignite your extramundane senses. You will always be forgiven. I can go on for days about the ways you complete me. I love you. I need you. The possible explanations as to why I need you are beyond moral reasoning. I will become a habitual lover. My dissertations will forever embody the elegance that noticeably surrounds you. I don't mind being the man you need. I can support you. No matter what this takes, I know you're worth it all. I plan to caress you nightly and often tuck you in bed. I draw you a bath, and maybe even much more than that. Truthfully, I would do anything just to see you smile. I'm positive things won't be easy; I have barriers built. I built them so as time begins to successfully progress, the walls will crumble. Could you stand by my side in my darkest times? I'm not asking you to stay through infidelity, but what about PTSD? Please don't leave when those nights come that I can't sleep. What about overthinking? Please don't leave on those days that we don't speak. What about anger? Frustration? Please don't leave when times approaches when you don't like me. Forgive me for the journey ahead because I don't know where these roads will take us. In love, I'll probably hurt you in ways I never mean to. Just have faith in our love and I know it'll all work out. If you can cherish this small light, then my light of a trillion stars will be worth the effort to stay. I need you. I'm what you call a gateway drug, these are the side effects of loving me. I will love you gently. I will be your supporter even when you're mad at me. I will love you through your darkest times; I will love unconditionally. I will hold you when you feel worthless and remind you that you're beautiful. I know you're not perfect nor are you the absolute best, but those aren't the traits that fill the dress. I plan to give this relationship all that I have just to gain some success. I need you to know that when you start to feel as though you can't; I'll be there to reassure you that you can and will. I am your number one fan. I am your King, your friend, as well as your man. I will unconsciously love you in the most remarkable ways possible. I think I'm in love with the fact that I need you. The wonders that invade my mind are feelings that subdue our love in mystical manners. Damn, I need you.

Genuinely, that would be my moral explanation on needing love. I can't explain it precisely because love can be different for everyone. As for me, I need love because it drives me insane. I love to go insane when it's for the right reasons. My mind can venture off to various realities if love is the priority. As psychotic as that may seem; love opens new levels of creativity, urgency, even vulnerability with another soul. The chance to have openness with another person is what I would go insane for. There will always be those who hate love; personally, I believe they hate it because being intimately involved with someone could end recklessly. Which is a valid feeling to have towards love. When it's not cherished love can end brutally which for most takes a lot more than they must give. I know there are people out there like that, but then again there are those like me, who truly don't care. I will hop in the driver's seat without a license nor experience and drive you insane because that is exactly what love does. It makes you dangerously strong. I would pick up the moon and throw it back at earth if it keeps me in love. I appreciate love because I'm not afraid of it. Even with all the unforgivable things that love has done to me; my need for love outweighs the pain. I feel incomplete without feeling love outside of myself. I want to wake up in the morning and know that love is beside me. I want to travel the world and see different outlooks of life with someone I cherish. I need love. Many times, I feel unworthy of something as authentic as love. Having love is rewarding, it's something we all need no matter how much we convince ourselves otherwise.

I would personally attest to the hardest thing surrounding love would be the maintenance. I fail effortlessly at communication, understanding, and trust. My egotistical mindset makes things considerably complicated. I feel as though, sometimes, I am most important because there's been enough times where I wasn't considered at all. Being in love helped me learn that selfishness must subside. The baggage you carry from earlier relationships should be released as you carry a cup full of new love. Unfortunately, you shouldn't place value on your new relationship based on the pain from any other relationship. When dealing with someone it's your duty to make sure you give them everything that you have. That would leave you in the position to trust that they'll give you everything in return. Figuratively, we all want love but being in love is too damn hard sometimes. I think we make love hard by bringing fear into our love life. We fear love's ability to fail. We grew accustomed to the constant failure in love, we never found healthy ways to keep it. I learned to admire love; therefor instead of guarding myself or fighting love, I embrace it. As humans we deserve love, so learn to do whatever it takes to keep it. Foolishly, that would mean it could potentially cut you but at least you'll bleed knowing you were madly in love.

C. U. T

The lacerations across my heart bleeds. They cut me so deep, after a while; you find the deepest secrets that hide within me. I feel defeated; beaten, destroyed, murdered so softly that now I rationalize the thought of losing you. Help me understand the importance of communication, understanding, and trust. I'd rather not lose you, but I need those three things to maintain consistency within our relationship. I'll do whatever it takes so guide me in the direction desired. In return, I'll learn to grow alongside you. You'll butcher my heart and I'll butcher yours. I'll teach you concepts that are never one sided. I adulate you. I'm delighted by your company; I even adore you. But I hurt you like those before me. Honestly, most times; I don't feel I am worthy to hold you in reverence. Yet my heart wants to see yours smile.

Being honest, communication is a vital part of any relationship. Opinionatedly, for a solid relationship, one must stand on communication. Many relationships experience failure because of their inability to communicate. Most people think that 'communication" means specifically talking to their significant other; it doesn't. Communication is much more than simply spoken words. The definition of communication is *the imparting or exchanging of information or news.* Communication is a plethora of things because you can exchange a long list of information in various ways. Why? Might I add; you can communicate with your eyes, words, hands, actions, even thoughts. This could exuberate you or even eradicate you; either way we all fail thinking communication is linear, we tend to think: "If I speak then they should listen and or respond because we're communicating." Every thought like that will always be wrong. Everyone's trauma is different, which hinders their ability to effectively communicate. Require yourself to find a commonality as well as an understanding within your communication; the benefits are rewarding.

Fairytales happen to exist when you're in a relationship. Together you are considered one; individually, two people a part of one whole. Hypothetically the relationship would be split up in percentages where together things are split 50/50 between one another. Chances are that there will be countless times where things aren't always equal. Although we're all human, there comes a time that we need to feel for each other so that understandings are accurate. There will come a time where our loved ones require us to give 75% of ourselves while they give only 25. Would it be too hard to communicate more than the person with the problem? What happens when they only have 10% to give? Could your love guide you through to that 90% they'll need in support from you? Trust becomes harder when understanding is all that you stand behind. Communicating to understand your lover is different because of communications excessive need. Learn to communicate further when you grow tired of talking for the strength of your love. Attempting to give someone the world is excruciating because it requires 100% of you; at the times they have nothing to give. That's love. Love requires you to do anything to stimulate your lover which includes understanding, intimate affection, peaceful patience, as well as sexual sensitivity. Love requires sacrifices. Therefore, communicating could mean not speaking when there is much to say. Learning the trait of trust eases your significant others mind. Consider trust the astounding unity between two minds. Understanding can be easily communicated in a sense because of trust. Communicating is typically being able to engage in whatever the other is engaged into. For example, your loved one is playing the game instead of talking to you. ENGAGE! After the game show compassion, it doesn't matter whether you truly care. It's for them to feel as though you care. Ask them about their interests, then actively listen. **ENGAGE IN INTELLECTUAL COMMUNICATION. LEARN TO UNDERSTAND ONE ANOTHER.** Don't fear overcommitting to understanding because there will be a day you need to be understood as well. Don't be afraid to speak your mind. All thoughts must be communicated in a way that you both gain a better understanding of each other. The most important thing when communicating is to gain a sense of understanding. Even though it's complicated it's still necessary for emotional support. Always communicate to gain understanding.

"Why can't you read my mind? What makes me so difficult to love? Am I too weird? What makes me different? Am I not enough? I wouldn't know, but things are tough. It's beginning to get to the point where I'm believing that I'm misunderstood." Those are just some of the many ways people cry out for understanding. We all deserve to be understood. According to certain statistics trauma can be severe in adults from adolescent ages. This correlated to understanding, despite age. A lot of us know what it feels like to be misunderstood.

Situational understandings aren't always bad. Being in love becomes much harder without understanding. The sense of understanding must be reiterated in the saying 'I love you'. We have to gently find understanding. Perhaps, tender proclamations aren't enough to describe genuine adulation, but still; we must learn the value of benevolence. Case in point; understanding, which could mean figuring the other person out by filling their voids with you. Is that truly possible? If it's impossible, then trust could never be present. Opinionatedly, can you say you're in love without those needs being fulfilled? In love the goal is to fill each other's voids with one another's existence. That's like saying: *"love I'm going to need you spiritually; mentally, emotionally, as well as physically."* Although moments will be hard; time will help strengthen understanding.

Understanding takes much more than communicating. Life is more profound than minimal words or expressions, therefore; perceive intelligence with meekness because there is excellence in open-mindedness. Learning how to emotionally embrace love dismantles the barriers between affection. We must work on holding each other in safety by considering security without a home your 'commitment.' The act of gaining understanding requires you too feed a hungry soul in various ways, starting with patience. Giving patience is pivotal in obtaining an understanding. As you learn yourself, find understanding in love itself; all the while learning your significant other. In retrospect, that's complicated. It screams that patience is important. Next would be vulnerability. When you are vulnerable it solidifies the acceptance of each other's individuality. Do things in a way that helps gain a mutual understanding with someone other than self. Remember; love lasts for eternity. Vulnerability allows that eternal flame to burn passionately. Take your time with yourself or a loved one and learn to comprehend the meaning of life. In return, understanding will last you both a lifetime. Lastly is acceptance. We all think. We all feel. A lot of things pertaining to understanding are avoided because none of us are easily understood. Therefore, learn to use endless advantages to understand each other. Understanding will take all that you have to interpret its true meaning. Even if you believe you have nothing to give, it'll take all your nothingness and turn it into something. Communication is valuable, because to communicate effectively requires positive understanding. Otherwise, the negativity could impact the relationships trust in ways that are inconsolable.

Overall, the concept of understanding depends on the person's perspective. Understanding yourself may create conflict; thereafter, make room to understand someone else. Closed-mindedness reinforces misunderstanding. When considering other beings don't be afraid to use imaginative understandings. Keep an open mind for all the possibilities that could happen when you love someone. Interpersonal growth allows every individual to learn their portion of the relationship's unification. Meaning for perfect harmony I can give my all for the sake of understanding. This is what I consider complete unison. Unison is only found when your heart is full of love, your mind is developing, and your soul ecstatic. Nevertheless, the question that will remain will be can you trust this?

"WE HAVE TO HAVE TRUST" The relationship will not last without trust. The relationship can grow with communication because it leads to understanding, but without trust the foundation fails. Trust as far as you can see, intentionally as well as indirectly. Once you say you're in love you are obligated to trust that they are in love with you. Believe in love! Otherwise, ask yourself; why are you in a relationship? Trusting serves as the most complicated part of love. Trust becomes obscure because of the amount of vulnerability it requires us to have. Trust also requires a higher level of sensitivity as well. The relationship can remain on one accord within the process of trust. A persistent sense of communication establishes a complete understanding. Therefore, it becomes easier to believe that your vulnerability is considered. When in love there are promises we don't always say aloud. The unwritten agreement is to grow together as one. When that seems hard, lose expectation and learn to trust someone to uphold their portion of the agreement. Notwithstanding mistakes, master the element of progression. Things will continually happen to two people taking the time to love one another. Respect loves standards, then demand a heart alignment. Realize that trusting each other takes time. No matter what comes against your love plow through it with pride. Desire better communication. Remain confident that with time you both will begin to understand each other better. Trust that no matter how far love takes you, they forever be beside you. Learn to believe in the words; *I trust you.* Those three words are just as hard, if not harder to say than I love you. It is okay to feel love. It is promising to have trust. Start with love then search for interpersonal understanding; they're essential to your growth. Trust that loving someone else begins with effective communication.

Accepting love forces you to trust. Once you believe it in your heart, communicate it with your mouth. It can begin with questions. Do you trust me? How could I trust you? It's reasonable to have multiple questions that need answers when you decide to trust love. Address the trauma you have faced vulnerably. This allows them the space to react respectively to the fact that it's scary to trust. As insane as it may seem in love, you must trust. We all know without it the relationship remains unstable, therefore find ways to be able to put your trust into someone else. Believe what is said with your entire heart. That is the only way to find an equal level of understanding together. The safest thing to do is put your past behind you. Once that openness is accepted and that vulnerability is respected an outpour of emotions can be articulated. I can trust you. I will communicate with you to gain understanding. Desire more than tangible successes. Trust that when you open the doors the path will lead right back to trust. Trust that you can be handled with the same amount of care you give. Welcome your loved one into your complicated life of crazy love. Which means if you truly want love then you will learn how to trust one another. Don't be afraid to say, *I trust you.*

Evaluating these three aspects helps support love. As a reminder, Communication, Understanding, and Trust are the most vital elements in any relationship. Communicating allows you to learn the language of your love. Expression allows a distinct avenue, which creates a direct pathway to understanding. Thereafter, understanding your loved one surrenders their heart in trust. Once the relationship has trust, a foundation is created for the growth and healing of hearts. Allow love to cut you no matter how deep because you will do the same to someone else. From experience I have learned it's easier to let your guard down and forgive yourself from your past life. Seek forgiveness throughout the relationship because you become unified in love. The trauma you faced before them has nothing to do with them, but it doesn't mean you can't love them through it. Love is astonishing in unity. The process of solid harmony is tough but learn to be pleasantly patient. People are delicate individuals with unpredictable emotions. Many people have exhausted every outcome and will overreact to certain situations. Just be patient with them. Patience is a virtue, so remain virtuous. The only way to maintain a relationships virtue is through the acronym "C.U.T" Each letter in the acronym has its own distinctive meaning. Are you in love and want it to last? Allow love to cut you; then grow from that with equal amounts of time and acceptance. The importance of each individual aspect entices the relationship's growth. For the sake of love: **study** your significant other, *learn them*; and acknowledge them. Just as companies label; cigarettes, pill bottles, medicines, even tools. This is the same warning label; everything begins and ends with communication; start by perfecting that aspect. The final two will follow along.

Happily, in love, I have experienced hurt. The exact reason anyone would be scared to love. **The dark side of love is vicious!** Eventually, spewing; venom, hatred and resentment at the same time. A romantic evening can become a fight at home. A conversation becomes a screaming match. Eventually, spewing; venom, hatred and resentment towards each other for no reason. Absurdly, trauma puts a limit on growth. **Communicate, Understand, and trust.** Each one of the three are tools that help you deal with love. There must be a willingness to understand any flaws. Deep unfiltered communication can be detrimental to any relationship. It is important to find better alternatives. Explore outcomes to improve on any situation. In the heat of any moment mistakes can turn into habits. Tension creates a trail that misery loves to follow for reasons beyond reasoning. Paths like that would make anyone overwhelmed with emotions. Love: light or dark, makes it hard to trust. A love that could end the next day with sorrow.

Love makes you feel empty with regret in mind. Throughout the many mistakes and tears, don't forget to grow. Finding love is already hard enough; *maintaining*, makes love complicated. Love can become a chore. Even still, once you find belief, you will understand faith. A hurt heart still has the space to heal. Be willing to take the cuts because you can begin to learn maintenance. Many people dream of obtaining true love but lack the knowledge to keep it. Preserving life teaches you the passion for gardening. Sustain the relationship in ways that may leave you bleeding out, alone, in love. ***LOVE REQUIRES SACRIFICE***. Progressive communication provides situational understanding, with peaceful trust. Unconditional love becomes the result of healing all wounds. In love, pleasantly speak with interest in believing the truth. "Communication. Understanding. Trust."

DON'T LEAVE

lease do not leave me! Although we're inharmonious; I don't want you to leave. *I am sorry.* I made mistakes but don't worry I'm growing. Ain't it funny how we beg our lovers to continuously put up with our problems? We beg for love then turn around and allow love to walk right out our front door. This makes me believe that most of us wouldn't know what true love felt like. Unfortunately, keeping love could become an occupational hazard. The shape of your relationship depends on the number of unselfish understandings that are shared. Ensuring that your relationship is not easily broken, requires more than most of us are willing to give.

Fight for love, more literally than figuratively. Love is worth every wound that never healed. Love is supposed to be unconditional, meaning; it is everlasting. Love equips us with the power to withstand adversity because *love conquers all.* When love doesn't conquer, don't lose faith in love; understand that you lose in love too. Love doesn't always mean you'll be happy. Love is frustrating; arguments with your lover can become consistent. Situations turn physically or verbally abusive, which makes fixing things more complicated. This would be the best time in the relationship to seek a spiritual connection with love. Once things steer too far out of your control it's safer to leave those things alone. The battle for love is the hardest because the pressure tends to make love less desirable. **Love will test you.** Which allows self-love to play the important role of guiding you towards peace. Love is more complicated than most would predict. A relationship will remain in balance with the right amount of encouragement. Things will not always be blissful but make sure you notice the collateral beauty. It'll be impossible to avoid an argument but at least they aren't detrimental. There will be time taken to make one another happy but it doesn't feel like a job. The time you spend together isn't as overbearing. Having a perfect balance with love takes years of trial and error, so don't give up so easily in the beginning. A love that lasts forever needs an abundance of patience, so if you're willing to try; the relationship will last.

Love is arguably complex because you could feel absolutely **"NOTHING"** and still be in love. Even still, love has such a wonderful feel. Especially when the person you love loves you back. Forgiving isn't where love is placed; it's forgetting. Love allows you to forget that the pain was as bad. Love forces us to free ourselves from the rejection we face in love. Don't fear opening your heart to the pleasantries of love. Be free. Even a heart of coal has a diamond underneath. Love teaches us purity. Love is one of the best teachers because we learn from our mistakes. No matter how naïve it may seem, love provides us with blind faith, a subtle result of unconditional love. When love is treated carefully, its waves erode the pain away. Never leave someone who finds the time to love you every day. Place your pride aside sincerely within the relationship. No matter how hard love gets, don't leave. Compassionately learn your companions love language. Don't leave without first admiring the intimacy mixed with desire. Don't leave until you've replaced the section full of pride with consideration. As exhausting as it could be it's important that the significance of love rests in all minds. Don't leave without expressing how amazing love has been every day. Don't leave withholding the lightness of someone else's being. Sometimes people need love to overcome their own mistakes. Darkness will always attempt to consume the lightness of being. Sometimes the fear of losing becomes the fear of loving. Some people aren't afraid of love because their hearts make those decisions; whereas, for others, fear allowing themselves to love someone because they'll leave. Don't leave without asking them not to leave you instead. Relationships become harder when everyone has their way. A heart of two souls beat as one when both desires are met. The past tends to hinder the future. Don't leave without realizing love connects you to yourself.

If you want the relationship to last, learn to outgrow your past. Accept what happened and grow into what's going on. The struggle in life becomes our past overbearing our souls. Take chances! Make sacrifices! Break down your past. Try to recall the pain implanted within your heart. Speak on the past as a reminder of the journey through love because relationships can cause PTSD. Speak to your significant other about all those things that caused you trauma. Learn to exist without fear. Allow them to whisper an opulent amount of love back into your life. **Let them motivate you. Let the heal you.** Let them love you. Let them into your heart so they can learn your vulnerability; ***but do not let them leave.*** Things are much harder when there's an immovable object of hurt between two lovers. **Learn to grow.** *In every aspect.* ***<u>GROW THE FUCK UP!</u>*** Love is replaceable when you easily lose out on someone who wanted to love you through everything. Love is the toughest opponent in Russian roulette. In the end you could be dead or feel alive, but it is love. Who cares? Why would you care? Love is irresponsible, that's why. Love is confusing which drives us all a little mad. Don't leave because the last person you allowed to hurt you is not this person. Find excitement in love. Find a warm spot beside their heart to love your pain away. Growth in love heals the heart from its traumatic past. Heal your heart by growing in love. Fuel your hearts fire and desires. **Grow in love.** Getting the best out of love starts with small talk. Every step of the way remember love is like night and day. Make love work despite the issues by understanding that love is always there. When things feel cold, find the space to keep love warm by learning from each other. Therefore, the best comes from love when you understand the needs with your relationship. Ask yourself are you wrong for loving so much? When does the relationship become worth everything you have to give? This is love. Love isn't a fantasy where you can add or subtract your wants and needs. Love is deeper than a singular thought; it's backed by action. **This is love.** Love will leave you destroyed. Love will leave you broken-hearted questioning your worth. Love will excite you and moments later send you plummeting towards the ground in fear. *This is love.* Cherish the fact that you're able to feel loved. Admire the fact that you've fallen in love. Embrace the mistakes you make within love and continue to find love. Love will leave you teary-eyed and ready to commit suicide while you're in love. Do not run from it. Don't forget about it; understand that this is all love. Do you have what it takes to keep love beside you, or will you leave?

Don't leave because you had an expectation of someone else. Although you gave all you had to give it's only a desire, nonetheless. Unfortunately, desires do not equate into actuality. If you gave your all in love, meaning; you changed into someone you're not, you created a new self-image for love. I commend you because from experience; it's hard. It's scary to give love all that you have because there's always a chance that love won't be returned. Learn to appreciate the pain because they aren't who you want them to be. They are exactly what you need them to be. In love you can place pride aside and they still find reason to leave. Don't leave amid a mess without making sure you take care of love. We're all broken and torn but those that desire love blossoms especially. Don't question if you'll make it through another heartbreak. Question how much you're willing to give for love. If things still end give yourself enough love to move on and take care of yourself. Closure is imperative because there are countless justifiable reasons as to why they might leave. We all deserve to know what we were left with hurt. Do not blame love. Don't turn your back on love because those you decided to love never loved you the same. Don't leave without understanding what love means for every individual. *Turn that frustration from heartache into understanding.* Learn to accept what was because it does hurt. Learn to grow into possibility because you never know what could happen. Continue to love even though you begged them not to leave.

THE BREAK-UP

The anguish that breakups bring leave countless hearts broken; some endings just aren't as good as the beginnings. Even on my worst days, I'll still choose love. I want the kind of love that's magical, where love prevails. I want someone's presence to supply the same amount of peace that the stars would. Do you think love could still be beautiful when things get ugly? Unfortunately, love has its dark moments. Those times where prince charming loses out on the princess. Life is not coincidental, it's unfair; knowing that every sacrifice made for someone could be overlooked. Heartbreak happens when the person we love doesn't love us back. The love that fuels relationships can come to a halt because after a while the relationship may never be the same. Many of us experienced firsthand the detriment of a heartbreak can cause various declines in the relationship. Nevertheless, it's the truth that we can't deny; *that love can fade.*

The test of love is one that your soul can't rid itself of. Allow the test to run its course but don't allow the test to ruin the love in your heart. We all fall in love, but some experience a love like no other. Then there are others; those who fall casually yet guarded because love hurts most when the other person decides to leave. The easiest way to maintain a broken heart is by moving on. Take the journey to seek a better version of self for the next relationship. Relationships can become harder as time progresses without the proper care. A relationship requires maintenance. Checkups. Whether it's a relationship with self or someone else; society loves to portray love as a magical feeling. They create these figments of what love should look like. They tell desirable stories about relationships that are rarely true. The love that's idolized in the media isn't the same as real love. *Real love is harder.* Love can be upright in your face hideous. Imagine times where venomous words and actions are followed by apologetic resentments. *That is real love.* Love can be a casual Saturday in the house spent cleaning and taking care of things for the following week. Love isn't always extravagant; the simple things should be cherished just as much as the most memorable things.

We as people tend to put up with things, we know we're undeserving of. Why are we okay with being uncomfortable for love? I think we forget that we have worth. Fortunately, we don't have to deal with anything we feel undeserving of. Believing that love conquers all results in forgetting our individual worth. Don't get me wrong we all want love to prevail but don't force yourself to feel worthless to try and make love work. Love lasts longer when it's taken care of, but love grows when both parties are fueling the love that's shared. As humans we are worth millions; an affirmation to never forget. No one can truly have you until you understand your self-worth. As much as this seems like a love between two people, the love you share with yourself works the same way. As life moves you must move forward with it. Whether you have a significant other or not you'll admire the love you had that's no longer around. I feel sorry for those who love hard; this journey in love won't be easy, *but it's worth it.*

Living happily and healthy without love is like fasting with just fruit, vegetables, and water for the rest of your life. It's already hard enough to go cold turkey from any meat because were born carnivorous. Once you realize that means; no sugar, no salt, no junk, these sacrifices begin to seem nearly impossible. All the varieties of food condensed into fruit and vegetables. Every drink that's out there turned into water. These sacrifices seem unnecessarily tough because there are no other options. Metaphorically, that's how I see breakups. How can you live happily and healthily without the options love brings into your daily life? Love makes you smile in the morning. Love makes you take care of yourself. Love rolls you out of bed and makes you sing effortlessly in the mirror at the start of the day. The pleasantries that love brings into your life are going to be missed when you think about saying **"FUCK LOVE"** with hurt in your heart. Start with deletion as which step to take first after a breakup. Those pleasantries can become unpleasant once it's all said and done. Delete everything about them out of your memory for you will spend a lot of your time reminiscing. The best solution is to *"feel"* the emotions to analyze the decisions made. Work on self no matter what's going on. A breakup. A newlywed. A divorce. It doesn't matter what stage you're in, always find the time to take care of yourself. Understand all the negativity that you were left with and accept the positivity you can take. Analyze the various situations within the relationship and question everything. Why do you feel this way? What was your role in all of this? These questions are important because they hold you accountable for the ways you feel. That way you can take care of yourself without the help of anyone else. Growth shows that someone could be worth more than you give. Reflect on your situations that way decisions mature progressively. Learn from one another for growths sake. Despite the outcomes in life use everything for grace. We must love each other so passionately that we learn about each other. The pain that heartbreak left you with molds your understanding of; signals, people, as well as yourself. As you grow from those understandings learn so you don't make the same mistakes. Things seem to usually end with one sided turmoil after breakups. Even if you were the one to break things off that doesn't make you right. We all have flaws, some fatal; but learning from the fatalities is the most important thing. Try not to be the same person you were for the last person you loved. Change for the betterment of self because you'll have to handle your broken heartedness yourself. Heartbreaks cause you agony. Heartbreaks tear you apart but face the emotions for yourself. Because a lot of things become water under the bridge after a while.

LESSONS LEARNED; BRIDGES BURNED

What happens next after losing the one you love? How does one recover from giving so much then disconnecting moments later? All the time lost. All the memories that are now faded. Sometimes we all begin to sulk, then a darkness tries to overcome you; but never succumb. The worry and doubt cannot fill your hollow vessel. Learning to love again is the best option in this world. Simply because, forgiveness heals the heart; whereas acceptance soothes the mind. Peace becomes necessary when things get too foggy because nothing is more agitating than a deep depression eating away at your soul. It begins to gnaw through your mind, for depreciation purposes. Rule number one is knowing that life is too short. It is important for us as people to learn the lessons we are taught; it's what grants us wisdom. Life is already scary enough but being depressed in this scary world only makes life harder. So now not only is it hard, not only is it scary, but you're also depressed as well. No matter how much you convince yourself that you're better off alone attached to pain, you're better off without it. You'll thrive in the light outside of the depressive darkness even if you're the only one to tell yourself that same thing. Remember self-assurance is the best reassurance anyone can give.

The day you meet someone you want to spend the rest of your life with, can be the scariest. No matter how badly we may want them they may only want us for the time being. They might put up with us for a little while but there's no way for sure to know that they'll be here forever. Does that make them any less than the person we met? Forever does not always last a lifetime. There are short-term forever's that last while you are in it. There are small lifetimes that only last until you realize you're worth more. That does not mean they're horrible people. It might just be a bridge that was burnt or simply a lesson that needed to be learned. It's on you to decide which category they fall in. Just like it's on you to choose the actions after categorizing them. We as people tend to lose ourselves in love. We search desperately for love, which in return leaves us alone in pain because love comes and goes but we are not always ready for the love someone must give. The problem I notice that most deal with is the fact that everyone won't deal with you in the ways you'd like to be dealt with. Everyone won't even see you as their equal let alone treat you as you desire. There are ways around this, but it's always overlooked. GROWTH. Some will see you as stuck up, some will even talk down on you, and if we're being honest here some will even disrespect you. At the end of the day, it's the fact that you're willing to grow that makes you stand out. It's the fact that you're willing to see beyond the daily blocks and attempt to seek greatness in times where it seems like it's nothing but failure. GROWTH is the biggest flex you could have over anyone. It's vital because people will remain the same then will try to drag you down with them. People are like crabs in a barrel. Once you seem like you can escape everyone will tug on you to bring you back down. Some would expect you to be strong enough to carry the whole barrel, once they realize you cannot, they'll step over you and leave you wherever you are. Humans weren't designed to agree and co-exist with no problem. Those kinds of things take time. Selfishness prolongs these matters but usually what's important to people is how they feel. Which is why some people can't follow you wherever it is you're seeking to go. These are the various reasons amongst many more that ruins relationships.

At the start of every relationship people tend to stand opposite one another. In some cases, the relationship may even start with so much in common, complete understanding, even ultimate pleasure. Relationships can start and remind us of the stars in the sky but whether it's time, love, or anything else. Holes begin to seep right in the middle of the structure of the relationship. The bridge that you guys are building to connect has gaps within it, some you'll circle back to. Others left as is, with hopes to replace them in the distant future. I believe that we often forget that's it's harder to forgive than to forget. We as humans can say whatever it is that we want to, but, if your loved one did something unforgiving 10 times over; it gets tougher to forgive. You might've forgotten the first couple incidents. Can't even recall how it all first began because you forgave them and forgot but once it happens that next time. Forgiveness is not what comes to mind. It's the question of how they could continually do these things and still say they love you. Questions start arising for them to answer but instead of asking them to offend them, you offend yourself. Instead of telling them how it's truly affecting you, those statements are heard less than the last time. Who do we blame? What can we say when we are building a bridge that's burning as we progress? How can one say they truly forgive their partners if the "mistakes" happen consistently? Is it still considered a mistake? We build these bridges with people through various things. Maybe its reciprocated energy. Sometimes it's thinking of them when they did not think you would. People even tend to build bridges based upon the time spent with one another. Those types of bridges burn, in all honesty; they're the easiest to set aflame. When I stated we're all human, those are the reasons. We bond together through emotions. Which is the biggest flame any human has. Emotions matter because the moment energy isn't reciprocated the relationship has questions. Is it fair? Personally, I don't think it's fair for any relationship because learning about one person will leave them emotionally scarred by the other. It is inevitable. No matter how hard we try to understand one another we're completely different emotionally. We are fueled differently by different emotions so if we build a bridge based on emotions the question won't be why did we allow it to burn, but why was it built in this manner to begin with? Bridges don't stand upright with a piece of every metal, all the screws out there, not even with every wire created. So why build a relationship based on every emotion… because they make you feel every emotion? No, you must build a relationship on things that stand between one another. A few examples would be trust, understanding, as well as considerations. Those are examples of pillars that give the relationship an agreement. Agreements stand while feelings change.

When couples agree they grow together. Even friends grow because both of you feel understood and respected. If I focus on how, you make me feel though I might truly dislike you. I could even hate you. You might've said something. You might've done something that truly hurt me. It really didn't boil down to complete disrespect, but it felt as though. We can't have a relationship on that. That isn't saying that the relationship won't have respect towards one another's feelings. It's saying that some things we must learn about each other, so respect one another's feelings. That's how you burn a bridge. It's not easy in no way emotionally. We are all guarded. Traumatizing times affected us all in life. Quite frankly I don't believe you can make it in life without trauma. Life will cause you trauma, leaving you face down deciding whether you're here. Do you feel paper thin, blowing in the wind; feeling like no one truly sees you. Trauma can leave you wondering but there must be understanding for both parties. There must be acceptance between anyone within any relationship. Trust is a solid factor, trusting someone matters most because it'll feel like they stole your secrets if they betray you. Once the bridge burns it's like picking up melted ice cream. Especially without forgiveness. Recovery without forgiveness is like work without pay; extortion. In life the presence of your loved ones is desired but not always accessible, forgive them ahead of time or you will find it hard to forgive them at all. Everyone is different, but it takes someone truly trying to grow to stand there and scoop the melted ice cream and refreeze it. When you care about a relationship you put forth every effort to make things right. When you care you also understand what it means to respect one another's feelings. Distance. Negative sensations. It takes time to learn to care for someone so pack patience. Sit back. Relax. Fighting one another only creates unnecessary space. Find ways to be happy with one another. Those who respectfully disagree; I understand your point of view. It is tough. Take those you lose out on as lessons. Learn the mistakes made with the various individuals and personally grow. Life will bring people into your life to teach you valuable lessons. Some people are not always meant to remain beside you for the rest of your life. Certain people hinder you, so…. GROW. Take the displeasures of life to recreate new beginnings. Too often people get mixed into their emotions, which in my opinion; blinds them from the truth. It was meant to happen because there was a lesson which was on the individual to accept or deny. When you grow, you are supposed to reveal the skeletons, remove the pain, and forgive yourself. It is so much to reveal in growth. Patience will keep relationships intact. There are many components of growth because relationships fail, you need growth to find your truest self. Growth as an individual helps the growth of every relationship. The one thing to remember is that no matter how many bridges burn in life you must grow into who you're destined to be regardless. Learn your lessons no matter how many bridges burn.

EMOTIONAL ROLLERCOATSER

No matter what, problems are inevitable. Sooner or later, we will all experience things that hurt so much, they're unforgivable. How can you deal with emotional distress? Staring into the face of detrimental heartache could turn any soul colder than 3 kelvins. Time heals all things with the proper steps anyone can overcome any adversity. Give time to your feelings as well as your thoughts. Both their opinions affect your daily life. Emotions are better expressed with passion instead of rationality. When dealing with life make time to speak emotionally about where you are and what you understand. It opens channels through to your heart for spiritual understanding. Hypothetically speaking; my girlfriend dumped me; here's how I feel.

"YOU HUMILIATED ME!!! The disrespectful misfortune that embodies my heart is piercing. I cannot comprehend the ignorance that entangles within your mind. I'd stand on a mountain top exclaiming the humiliation you made me feel, but somehow; I respect you. I don't destroy your image; I only fracture the frame. I thought I gave you more than enough. I sought out religion to be near you because I thought you'd bring me joy. My pride was trampled on, meanwhile my heart was strung up. I turned into your harp worried about more than misfortune. I loved you. I adored you. I admired you. I thought

you were a blessing in my life because I grew up with you. I grew to love myself more than I loved you. I made you stronger even when I felt weak. I ignited the very flame that intensifies your being. I learned to love me by loving you effortlessly. Did you really love me? I do not think I love you. The hate in my heart is as intense as dreaming of our times together. I am afflicted. We had everything. I'd give you anything, but you desired so much more. I don't know why I gave you anything. This cycle only drove me insane. I lost the will to love another because I loved you so much. I don't remember you ever finding yourself in retrospect of me. Truthfully, you behaved like there was no hope for *US*. It was imperative for us to build but we're so good at destroying. We were only supposed to love but we only found new ways to hate. We never took the time to appreciate the love that we shared. Now I learned not to cherish things in hibernation periods. But don't tell me you love me. That will only confuse me more. Please don't tell me you need me because I require all of you. I need every part of you, and that includes your time. That's what makes love so hard to find. In the end I nearly just wasted my time. I thought you loved me. I thought the ways our eyes locked foretold the legacy of me and you. Everything always rushed back when you cross my mind. This could possibly be torment that I deserve for thinking about you. I got to get you out of my mind. I can't help but to think of the times I humiliated myself for you. I remember the cheating, the fighting; the pain we couldn't hide. I still question how I could love someone that doesn't truly love me back. I forgave you because I was too insecure to leave. I had this false sense of hope that one day you'll *learn* to love me. You never did! The countless years of loving you! The endless years of forgiving you! Those sleepless night mistaking your choices for accidents trying to love you through whatever. Honestly, you had to love me. I don't know how I live and know that I loved you so naïvely. By the looks of how you treated me, you despised my being. I remember the day you and your friends laughed at me, after you metaphorically; spat in my face. I knew deep down you didn't care about me. I just tried to save face. What about the time we promised to be honest about infidelity? I laid out all my problems because I wanted us to work. I only wanted to understand fault. Why did your friends matter more than I could? Loyalty stands for nothing when I can hardly trust you. We don't even communicate let alone understand the war between us. Tell me, did you love me? Help me! I'm running out of ways to blame myself. There are literally no options left to pin as my bad. There was only one thing I ever wanted from you. Remember? I asked you to stay by my side to be there for me. Tell me; *were you ever there?*

I can't fully blame you though; I'm not perfect. I replaced effective communication with screams. Sexually you weren't all I desired. I became so focused on myself; I couldn't see my wrongs. I blame myself for letting things get out of hand. I could've learned some other ways to solve problems. Our situations were invited to stay at my place. I was wrong in a lot of ways. I believe that I *do*, love hard. I think that I *am* self-centered. Maybe I *was* selfish. There's a possibility that I *have* expected too much. I wanted the world to *revolve* around me. Instead, I learned that our worlds meant nothing. I take responsibility for my problems. I was wrong for making you feel that way, and for that; I'm sorry. I don't know, maybe things could've worked.

Funny thing is I remember you felt embarrassed when you let out a fart or two. I can recall a moment in time when you saw the stars in my eyes. I thought of you as; everything. The strength your words gave me, made me feel like a King amongst men. Those moments I felt weak you were my pillar of strength. I relied on you. I wanted a love that was not easily broken. The impact you had on me will be forever remembered. Maybe ending things wasn't the best. I still think about you. I remember when you would hug me and whisper greatness into my ear. I haven't felt great since the day you left. I don't take pictures anymore; maybe I'm depressed. This is the poison your love has left my heart infected with. I'm so confused about all of this I don't know where to start. *Were you the one for me?* I don't understand why I feel these ways. I need you. Please grant me closure; don't I deserve that?

Maybe you were the monster, I only saw a Queen because love blinded me. I never understood love until we broke things off. After asking myself a bunch of questions, I finally reached the conclusion. Love was more than words, feelings, actions, or emotions. Love is each and everything that we do. Love was the night I drove around drunk and mad but ended up in an accident. Love was those countless nights you prayed for someone to see my potential. Love was those times I held your hand as we drove around the city. Love was you; it wasn't your name, but it was what fueled you. Love is what hurt me. All of that was love. Maybe you did love me. Truthfully, there might've been a time where you loved me, but I'll question why it faded. I guess it's safe to say I'm hurt. The only emotion I could acknowledge is hate. I can't fathom saying I hate you, but I hate how I feel. I hate how things happened. I hate a lot of things, but you; I could never. Could you tell, I still adore you? This was a move that benefited our long run the most. We needed control because all we did was hurt each other worse over the years. We did not appreciate what we had. Now, we have nothing. I didn't cherish you and you lost respect for me. We tore one another hearts to shreds, you hurt me so much. Somehow, all I want is you. I hate everything about us ending; but I can't hate you.

When in love or coming out of love; it's important to know where to go from there. The sadness is needed to carry on through love. Although this seems like the end, the journey doesn't begin and end with people; they originate from you. Once you experience a heartache, how do you recover? The answer would be felt emotionally.

Every individual makes decisions based upon their own moral codes. Handle each situation differently by respecting the emotions felt. Even if that does mean hate. Morally we are the ones that decide our own fate, but when it comes to love that fate is unpredictable. Love makes us crazy. Love can turn you into a heartless creature that hates love. Be careful when you love someone because a lot of us don't know enough about love. Love is convincing. It can convince you never to feel again. Love is dangerous. Those who result to hate after love, just patiently heal. All wounds require time to overcome. Focus on the pain that beats within your heart. Remind yourself of the fears that loving brings. Recall the hateful anger that festered in your mind, then, flourish. Learn to dictate the rate in which misfortune schemes. Don't allow the misfortunes to dictate your motives. Take the time to understand that everyone won't love as much as you do. Face the man in the mirror and remind yourself that it's okay to lose in love. There is no issue in hating someone for causing you pain. Remind yourself that the hate you feel won't consume you but fuel you to learn how to love once again.

I HATE YOU

How does one normally feel after a breakup? Naturally, I think everyone would say their fine to save face. We're all this warrior lover who has been hurt by love but it's only for the time being. When in truth we're hurting on the inside. Don't hide the emotion. Express it freely because it's felt. Be honest and say, my soul feels evaporated, my heart is shattered, my body feels abused, and my mind feels altered. Open your heart enough to say that you can't feel anything but hate now. Even though you rather keep things cordial, be honest about how you feel. Reality is scary, especially after breakups; all you have is yourself in the end. Emotions are meant to be felt. Confusion comes in between most emotions. It's okay to be hurt and feel hate, but not want to hate.

How could someone consciously destroy another someone without recalling the trauma they left? Love is a bit careless like that. Dedication is never an insignificant effort. Some, earlier than others; realize that, soon the love that's given won't return. Love isn't always reciprocated as we'd all wish. I think that's what hurts the most, dealing with everything love entails; just for it not to be appreciated whatsoever. The journey between "us" slowly turns into a separate journey for "me" and "you". The love will equate into loss. The love can turn into hate. Handle every emotion accordingly, because; everything that's felt is acceptable. Respectfully, don't feel bad for hating them. Remember they broke *your* heart, so, if you happen to feel anything negative; stand firm in every emotion. Afterwards, learn to ignore the various sentiments that creep into your mind about them specifically. Place enough value on yourself so that your feelings matter to yourself. Despite how disheartening life gets, you still matter.

Find peace in losing. That goes for anything; a partner, your best-friend, a family member, even a dog. Love does not make anything stay; there's always a chance they will leave. As a result, people become full of hate. At some point, a certain amount of loss can turn into hate. Just as life evolves a caterpillar into a butterfly so can a hopeless romantic turn into a heartless menace. Contrary to popular demand, accountability serves as the truth in a peaceful manner. The transition from being in love to falling out pushes every soul towards hate. Heartbreak enables people to place blame everywhere but onto themselves. Despite who's to blame there's always room for accountability. Even if you're holding yourself accountable for your actions; that is the proper way to hold yourself accountable. This is what I call placing *"personal blame"*. Believe it or not there are some things we all do wrong in each infringement. The feeling of losing someone you love couldn't be described as hurtful. Losing someone is a stab wound to the chest that just won't heal. Unfortunately, that's love; it hurts but the pain hurts much worse once you're out of love. *That's love.* **FUCK LOVE. I HATE IT.**

I hate love, it's such a worthless emotion. I can't stand the fact that I must start over, knowing that I never wanted things to begin in the first place. I was afraid; worried at night. I had to convince myself that you loved me. I told myself you were the one for me, but you never showed me. Were you ever? Did you really love me?

"Why was my heart and my mind was attached to the thought of you every night? Not only my heart but my soul as well as spirit too."

I still have love for you as crazy as it may seem, but now I hate you for all those memories spent loving you. I can't stand the moments that made me believe you'd be my wife. I can't stand any thought that surrounds you. Even though I can say I hurt you; my hurt is the pain that came from loving you. Your love was intoxicating, it made me insane. Tell me, what sane man would chase a woman across the country moments after he's been rejected? We sometimes lose our mind searching for love in the wrong places. The pain lovers can reign on one another carry enough firepower to fuel World War 3. Do you know how much pain you cause each other? In love there is adoration, but later the hate replaces all the memories and satisfactions. No matter what was needed in love, forgiveness was endless. Then, I cared, but *now* I hate you. My heart exclaims my brokenness loud enough to speak to seven continents. I hate this feeling that sits raw on my heart. It's more damaging than a virus, its cancerous. I hate you so much *now* because of the amount of love you made me feel **then**. *That much love took more than courage and effort; more than pride or understanding, IT WAS EVERYTHING!* I loved you **then**, now I hate you. The crazy thing is what you did to make me hate you wasn't as bad as the other things; it was quite simple. That's why I hate you, the simple stuff; because the most complex, foolish, inconsiderate, erratic, disrespectful, insanely odd difficulties were the easiest to deal with. *Then*, I was madly in love with you, **now I hate** *you*.

Tell me what's harder to handle, loving despite the pain they bring or recovering once you are all broken up? Hating allows you to release the negativity you feel but only to understand it; not to consume it. Love will take your heart through a list of emotions. Hate is one of them. Listen to it. This helps you learn the functional difference between the **HATE** you feel and the **LOVE** you feel. Once you allow emotions to dictate your actions, they mix your mind up. Looking to replace a love we once had a taste of, knowing it's irreplaceable. Lingering emotions compete with the freedom of your spirit which results into a bunch of confusion. Mistakes happen when the truth becomes misunderstood. Failure overcomes our being because we cannot understand the emotions we feel. When confusion takes part of the whole remember the mind is something you still control. No matter what clouded judgement brings dark days you can see the brighter side of things. Love can bring confusion because we all think that just because we give someone our all we deserve their all. Things become confusing because that's not always the case. Love is frightening because it can ruin you with just enough room. Just as having too much hate leads you to harsh realities; a life nobody's prepared for. We all know addiction is a real thing, but my belief is that love is a gateway drug. Love is the most addicting yet painful of all. When heartbreak occurs, it makes the addiction much worse. The sense of love and potential brokenness has now infested your mind and confused you on what love really means. We do not realize being addicted to another soul could lead to a recovery process none is spiritually prepared for. Even though people say tears don't help, they do! These natural releases and recoveries heal you in loving. These constant reminders that its okay too feel, shows a sense of self-worth. They heal the broken parts to allow you to display your strength. Those tears you fight back are worth every effort to push out. Pain doesn't end or begin with heart surgery. I would think if you were awake, it would change things. That shit hurt. Pain like that makes you hate every other soul; it could turn you soulless. With no hope. Being awake during surgery could drive you insane. Having loved someone unconditionally, for them to love you conditionally; how does one recover from that? Pain ends when you take a step back from forgetting about love. That's where the pain ceases. When searching for the remedies for a broken heart, it's not many options in love.

I'm sick and tired of being a welcome mat for love. This could be karma or the fact that I don't know how to love properly. Whatever it is, I hate it; I don't deserve to feel any brokenness within me. Despite the hateful venom I spew, I still want her presence. I'm madly in love with them. I want their being to make me whole because I never lost love. It's confusing. I want my hate to showcase in a way you feel pain. The exact pain that was left for me to deal with. I wish you could hurt just as bad as I am. Why did I choose to love you? I don't even know what else to say or do because of how much hate I have for you. I can't seem to figure out in my mind what to do. I know that I hate that I love you, but I also love that I hate you. Once hate consumes me I probably will never forgive you. Despite my choice the journey out on the ledge only goes two ways, so it's on you to choose your remedy.

REMEDIES FOR A
BROKEN HEART

When you spend so long on the edge, you're bound to fall off. In other words, when you've felt enough pain; eventually you will go numb. This sense of numbness is what I consider the direct pathway to the end. Numbness occurs when something traumatic happens and you fight or run from the experience. This defense mechanism makes us all go numb. Love sends you directly to the numbing state to protect itself from further damage. Even the sweetest thing can become bitter to the taste. Yearning for love comes at that depressive price. One moment can be the most blissful while the next is the most devastating. Addictions have very high prices; God tests and the devil tempts, so be sure to recognize the differences.

We get so lost in love that we must forget the idea of them. Everyone copes differently. Once love grows colder; everyone starts get lost in themselves. There may not be a specific way to handle a loss, but there's an unhealthy means to an end. Most of us find peace in habitual indifferences, without finding peace within; which results into a loss. We'd rather choose to hate over loving for a lifetime. I didn't expect love to hurt me so much that I resorted to things for healing. Not people. Not religion. **THINGS.** Tangible *things* that could recreate my circuits and throw me through a loop of emotions I'm ignorant to. How can I successfully cope without understanding?

Truthfully, we find our true selves in the bottom of different bottles; blunts, and canisters. We abuse these nouns to the point we alter ourselves. Once altered, consequently; it takes longer to find who we truly are. Therefore, the nouns; become your proverbial crutches'. People, places and things. Whether it's your friends, or parents; a substance, the crutch is demoralizing enough to make you dependent. These nouns don't begin as habitual substances. The subtle attempts at using a crutch became your excuse as to why you *depend so much on it*. When you grow dependent you tend to become functionless without the substance you abuse so much. As for people, you needed to be under that person so much you couldn't handle your business. As for a drug, like love; you need to feel like you were floating without a parachute. That first fall hurts like hell. Being in love, we believe with every fall someone should be there to catch us. Gaining experience in life, teaches us that some falls will leave you bleeding out; alone. There's no love left in a predicament like that. Some nouns are healthy, the goal is to allow the good ones to last the longest.

Socially, we're all noticeably broken. That six-letter word is the destructive force that pushes expiry. Being broken opens your eyes outside of therapeutic representation. We tend to debate about the positivity that surrounds substances that we deemed as better remedies for ourselves. When truthfully, the substance + the thoughts of my brokenness created desirable hallucinations. In other words, I forgot how things hurt. Nothing compares to that high of nothing, feeling like no pain exists. That noun made you feel tall while everything around you made you feel small. We all need something to fill those voids of life left in our hearts. We all need a piece of peace no matter how it's gotten. Even if that means at the beginning or end of every day. These remedies will be there for you at every turn which usually stems from something traumatic. Those experiences lead you to your own failures. Once you allow people to ruin your life, it's usually because of the ones you're closest to. Hurting from emptiness would drive any man to a substance that would fill the void. Even if it was momentarily; using anything excessively creates a codependency. Despite how hard life becomes trauma makes us all vulnerable. Therefore, in pain we shy away from love, because there's no room for love that doesn't love me back. I can't trust anyone because everyone always lets me down. I can't stay sober because I'm going insane, and one push could lead us into a suicidal situation. I'm a ticking time bomb with nothing but substance abuse to mend my broken heart. A known fact is that all substances make us feel invincible. The strength that fuels that feeling is backed by your brokenness. There will always be better alternatives, you must be ready in case any fail. When dealing with brokenness, if one plan fails leave room for a plan B.

First and foremost, don't obtain habits that cannot be backed financially. Would you rather see a healthy alcoholic or poor one? Seriously? Secondly, seek the betterment of your own self. That's most important. Lastly. Find a spiritual elevator, without that spiritual lift the rest of you will crumble. There must be a belief that things will see brighter days. Habits aren't always bad for you. There's nothing wrong with leaning in search for support. If it's used in moderation, learn to give yourself free time. But, also, remember to handle your business but also give yourself habitual time as well. When having habits, healthy, or unhealthy, have the finances to protect your demand for the said substance. That means keep work. Keep a job. How can you deal with a life or a heartbreak without a constant distraction? If you always stay still, thoughts will have ample time to pass through your mind. Don't confine yourself to the walls of your home, find something steady to build upon. Support yourself within; seek the betterment of your own self. Support yourself and or your excessive need for an expensive habit.

Mental health is important. People tend to take suicide jokingly, but you never know how close someone is to the edge. Impact people with love because being nice pays off. It's complicated to stay happy or motivated about a life that seems to drive you insane. God didn't place us in heaven or hell, as complicated as it may seem; he placed us somewhere in between. We were left here to fend for ourselves deciding what's best for ourselves in this life. That's how hectic life is for everyone on earth. Life was designed to tear down the strongest soldiers, because it's about your soul. Strength isn't always what you want to display. What about integrity, pride, even confidence? Things get dark in life but learning to navigate through the latest nights helps develop dignity. Things can turn for the worst in a matter of seconds, but it's the tough times that define you. For example, Michael Jordan wasn't defined by his regular season feats. It was the stellar play come playoff time. It was keeping finals series down to only six games. It was winning every final appearance that made him great. It's the man that shows his face when those lights are the brightest. Life will always force you to navigate in the dark. It's the battle between you and life for you to prove that you won't back down. When life throws a curve, you'll politely send it flying 503 feet in the opposite direction. The goal is to learn how to stare defeat in its face and proclaim progression, then succession follows. Decree it and declare it, so it shall be. Life is designed to test your strength, wills, faith, and beliefs. Life will force you to become Michael Jordan in the finals. Do you have what it takes to withstand the most discouraging moments in life? Do you know how to remain sane when you're rollercoasting full speed into the depths of insanity? That's what will define you. Character development allows you to grow for the betterment of yourself.

I usually notice that people don't know themselves spiritually. Which allows them to fail at being in complete harmony because the one impacts the whole. For those that don't believe in God, that's you. Use another medium. For those that are firm believers, understand this one thing. "God's Not Dead." I speak as a converted atheist. No matter what, God is there to help you in your toughest times. What may seem like your lowest moments still has enough space for God to be in the midst. He hears your cries and is always by your side. The battle is not yours it's the lords, therefore; trust in him. Keep learning and growing with thoughts of peace. No weapon formed against you shall prosper. Once you believe that, the stronger you will become. Believing in something bigger than you, speaks life into your soul. Sadly, the issue is in belief. That's where the real battle begins. He tests you for you to prove your worth to him. If you can't believe in anything else believe that God is amid everything. God has his hands all over the life you will live. It's called God's plan. Lift your spirit. Take care of yourself. But remember, don't allow misery the blessing of your company.

GOD WHY!?

When you place too much power into God, you tend to forget the power he has bestowed upon us as individuals. Throughout this book there have been countless experiments. I've allowed you as the reader to feel and think without consequence. I have allowed you to fuel your own; heart, mind, body, and spirit simply because I am not God. I am a doer of many things, but judging isn't something I'm good at. Learn to fuel your heart with what's necessary, the power is placed upon you as the individual.

Remember, after the break-up, we decided it was best to hate the opposing party instead of loving and forgiving. For good reason might I add; the hate stands in the way of the emotional sentiments. How is it possible to feel something for someone who doesn't love as hard as you? The best answer is to allow God to deal with them. God shall inflict his will on those spiritually; but don't interfere with what God has in store for you both. A lot of us are selfish in the way that forces God to be on our time schedule. As a result, those people will always feel they're receiving the back end of God's blessings. When truthfully; he's amid any and everything. God keeps an eye on all his sheep, which makes him our shepherd. We fail every time we think we're in this life alone. Life as well as everything within it; are created, powered, and continued by God. Believe in God throughout all moments in life. We all have our own opinion on who or what God is to us. Therefore, please don't take this as me forcing any religious acts or understandings onto you. I'm informing you of the spiritual sense. From my perspective, we have a spirit that's fueled and can be destroyed. It's very important that we learn what it takes to refuel that soul of ours.

Picking apart your daily lives spiritually requires honesty. Think back throughout the book; when everything failed why did you choose hate? Why did you choose substances? Why wasn't your soul important enough to call out to God? We as people tend to forget the impact our souls have. God wants your decisions to be supported by him. He wants you to choose him in the darkest moments and lay all your worries at his feet. The God you believe in should provide you with the abundance of life. This deity should be the answer to your questions in life. Name a God that asks for all your cares and concerns to then turn around and fail you? God will always provide his people with the guidance necessary. Win, lose, or draw God has always been in the midst. Why do we expect God to help us instead of hurting us in the moments where we hurt ourselves? Digging deeper, think about how much we blame God instead of ourselves for our individual mistakes. That's what I call human nature. We all need someone to blame because it's no way that all these things that happened in life can always be our fault. That sense of entitlement will always bite back. Learn to place pride aside to realize that sometimes you can be, will be, and usually are wrong in numerous instances.

Spiritually, have you tried to find peace within your chaotic mind? I think the complications appear within the search of situational peace. We must be at peace with our surroundings before we can be at peace spiritually. For example, when matters get clumsy in life; we stare into space placing blame on the creator. *We all fail somewhere but blaming God or anyone rather than yourself is the biggest failure of all.* We must find peace within our situations before we can find peace within ourselves. This is by far the easiest task, but situational peace requires you to place whatever you think as well as feel to the side.

This kind of peace requires an abundant amount of reflection; simply because you must look at every situation and see it for what it is, i.e., a breakup. We must understand that either one or both parties no longer wanted the relationship. Harsh reality; but it's the situation at hand. Afterwards you must learn to understand what happened. Usually, for some; that's the longest part of this process. Very few people like to dive deep into their own issues to seek the understandings of their wrongs; therefore, they tend to place blame. This is the reason why most people cannot obtain the understandings God has in store for them. God has an individual plan for us all and along the way another soul becomes intimately involved. Without the proper spiritual preparations, God will not bless you with your soulmate. Your love life didn't fail because of God; it failed because you weren't ready for love. Things like this hurt because we want people to stick beside us no matter what, but everyone isn't equipped to struggle with you. Some people aren't willing to cross burning sands with you on their backs. It's hard to move a stubborn mule, so imagine an unequipped soul that lacks the spiritual understanding to love another correctly. Always remember that you have two heads and one heart that connects directly to your soul. Which means, a head fueled with negativity will leave your heart and soul unfulfilled because the darkness never prevails.

In my opinion, blaming God for the negativity we all face in life; is ignorant. God saves us daily and we blame him the second we aren't saved. Life throws insurmountable curves for you to trust that he is always there. For some, including myself; God has saved me from suicide, prison, fatal car accidents, all kinds of life-threatening situations. There were many times I couldn't say anything, but God. I would be foolish to blame him for a failed relationship. Instead, I learned to thank him for those situations he brought me out of. I also think that complicates things because how are we ever sure that we left something alone for the better? Couldn't things have changed at some point? With God, if things were meant to be it will be done. That's why I believe that he's always protecting and providing. I remain open to gain more spiritual and situation understanding. In all things I think the bravest question to ask ourselves is how can we grow spiritually?

What's important is understanding the differences between good and evil. These two forces will come against you repeatedly. Once you understand the areas in between, the grey areas become obvious. Life comes at you fatally some days, but our outlook on our own lives will fuel our souls forever. For example, if you wake up in a light mood the events of the day will change based upon that. God wants us to be prepared for the battles we will face daily between good and evil. That's what life boils down to. The complications arise when the positive days are overrun with negative situations. We must understand that through adversity the person we become defines us better than those easy days. The way we handle pressured situations is the driving factor in success. So, tell me; why wouldn't you want positive success? Take a heartbreak for example, the realities of the relationship failure are the dire need for spiritual growth. Maybe they weren't for you right now, but trust that if God has a plan; it will come back around. Therefore, if this situation was supposed to remain strong then no storm will ruin the relationships success. Spiritual understanding doesn't require knowledge about God, it requires knowledge about you and the world that surrounds you. Once something negative happens we tend to speak negatively to our spirits. Learn to find a light within the dark moments. Smile throughout the day knowing that scars heal instead of being traumatized. Learn to forgive and forget. Don't allow the downfalls to keep you from going uphill in life. Push through and triumph over misfortune. I think God wants us all to believe that success is always on the other side of failure. Remember that no matter how dark or empty life may feel God still supports us; just trust him. God's love will always be enough. When the time comes, we must accept when we are not okay. Situations may come hard with little to no remorse, remember, but God. We must learn to accept situational understanding, meaning you must understand the difference in separate situations. This will not be easy. One must have spiritual understanding as well as situational understanding to decipher each aspect to gain total understanding. With God, no matter what life throws at you; you can gain peaceful wisdom in all your issues. Even when you fail, it's the choices you make afterwards that define you; not the failure itself.

FORGIVE AND FORGET

"Forgiveness?! Do you know what I've been through? Can you fathom the individual discontent this disconnect has brought to my life? You mean to tell me I must have forgiveness? You must've forgot... They hurt me. They don't deserve my forgiveness. My remorse. They deserve hell in gasoline drawers. Not love from me."

Have any of us ever felt this way? You know boiling over with discernment in the darkest of ways. Willing to spit fire at the abusers who left their victims in agony. Disintegrate their being because who grants them acceptance anyway? That's at least how most of us feel in the beginning of all hurts. It's not fair for one to have to be emotionally scarred by someone they thought, wouldn't. It's not okay to leave someone who never dreamed of leaving you, but tell me what can you do? People will walk in and out of your life if you grant them allowance, but in the end how can you stop them? People won't walk all over you, they'll never be able to disrespect you to your face, they even act so friendly it'll seem like you guys go way back. All and all people can't be controlled by you. You will not be able to stop them if they decide to leave. It's a harsh reality. The statistics behind it all are frightening but if someone wants to leave your life; let them go. The hardest thing we may ever have to do as humans is let go of people who do not belong in our lives. Open your mind to realize that you're better off without a lot of people and the problems they bring. If we're being honest, how could you forgive someone that cares less about how you'd feel? How can you forgive someone for intentionally hurting you? The question wouldn't be can you, but more so how long will you. Forgiveness doesn't just arise out of thin air, it takes time. It takes releasing those harbored emotions to have room in your heart to forgive. Take the time necessary to grow from the hurts otherwise they'll fail in every relationship thereafter. Understand the situation for whatever it's going to be; learn to accept it then deal with it. That's how you start the path towards forgiveness.

Everyone doesn't deserve forgiveness immediately; some things are harder to accept than others. Show forgiveness to those who you can forgive. In many instances people grant forgiveness with hate in their hearts for past traumas. When there's things you can't forgive, you must forget. It may not always be necessary to forget certain things but when it comes to the emotional discomforts, those things are better off released. Forgiveness is hard if you're constantly reminded of the pain, they've caused you. Forgiveness comes specifically from the heart for every individual. In order to forgive, you must first accept them into your heart. We're all human, and yes; some mistakes are worse than others, but we all deserve to be forgave. No matter how big or how small the situation may end up being we all deserve to be forgiven. That doesn't mean that someone can crash all your cars and you just forgive them and act like nothing is wrong. No. You're not a robot; you're human. Maybe the mustang crashing was easier to forgive than the Mercedes. No matter the circumstances, we all deserve a chance at forgiveness. We are all a tad bit selfish and that's the sad reality. We often experience some of the same things we put others through. However, most would point out how wrong someone else was for doing the same exact thing. Learn to forgive as if you've done what it is that you're forgiving someone else for. It's okay to disagree; fight, even separate for some time because of the circumstances. Nonetheless, seeking forgiveness begins when you can accept the wrong but not place fault. Funny thing about blame is that you can blame everyone, but it takes a real one to understand right from wrong. No matter how right you are; never treat anyone wrong. Selfishness ruins so many relationships because people are too stubborn to apologize for misunderstanding the mistakes made. Forgiveness starts in your heart because we know this may not be the last time, we're just too selfish to accept that most times. Allow yourself the space to forgive just simply because you'd want someone to forgive your wrongs. Otherwise, we'd live in a world full of outcasts. Nobody is perfect; so, a mistake is easily made every day. Some people just learn to forgive more than others.

What happens when the situation resides in my mind? How do I let go of the hurt someone else caused me? Forgetting the memories engraved on your heart or mind is a tough task. Grief grabs ahold of our soul and walk with us until we no longer feel sorry for ourselves. It takes time to forgive yourself, and even more time forgetting what happened. Either way, Forgiving and forgetting goes hand in hand. Although it seems impossible it is far from that. It starts with holding yourself in reverence. Having a certain amount of respect for yourself will make you want to forget. Who wants to remember how silly they were; in love, to be vulnerable enough for a heartbreak? Holding yourself to a standard above self-doubt. That's important. When things come against your character don't waste your time trying to repaint the visual. Understand that things happen for reasons beyond our control but it's not our job to hold a grudge. It's not our duty to make sure we never forget how we felt. The feeling may never be forgotten but it doesn't need to be a constant reminder either. We as humans take traumatic memories and use the emotions to build barricades to protect ourselves from feeling the same way twice. In the midst, we remind ourselves of that exact feeling, constantly. For what? Are you reminding yourself of pain so nobody else can hurt you? Love yourself enough not to intentionally hurt yourself; it's a reminder that you are someone you love as well. You too can grow resentful towards yourself for various reasons. Be careful with self because you too, can grow resentful and unforgiving towards yourself for many reasons. Forgetting nor forgiving is easy because it doesn't leave room for you to self-sabotage. Forgiving and forgetting is for the individual not for those that caused the pain. Learn to forgive and forget so that you're not constantly reminding yourself of the pain that has shaped you. Take back control over your life by forgiving those that hurt you and forgetting the pain they left you with.

This will not be easy but it's imperative that we all forgive and forget for our spirits sake. The last thing you want is to look back on your life and blame your past or yourself for your actions. It's one thing to make mistakes and it's another thing to make excuses. Don't excuse yourself from life. Handle the trauma by forgiving and forgetting. For example, you can't appreciate a newfound love remembering the issues from your last lover. You can't appreciate the life you're living today reminiscing on the past. Meditate. Find peace within yourself, then find the time to forgive and forget. People hurt you because they were hurting themselves. "Hurt people; hurt people." That will forever be a truth in many matters, therefore; it's safer to forgive, than forget. Don't ignore it. Don't avoid. Life has a fancy way of repeating the things you try to walk away from without confrontation. It's called karma. It'll come back and haunt you until you confront it with intentions of dealing with whatever it may be. None of us are experts on life but this is a lesson you can pass down to anyone. Holding grudges makes your heart smaller. Not scientifically, but theoretically you are draining yourself of the love you must share. Cowering behind hurt hoping it doesn't come back. Pain is inevitable. Hurt comes in so many forms. Don't pick and choose the types of pain or hurt you'll accept in your life. Learn to adapt to all facets of hurt so that you can withstand trauma. If there is a chance to avoid the situation altogether by all means, make it to where you do not have to forgive or forget. Avoid certain situations. Remove yourself from certain conversations. Take the time away from certain crowds. The goal is to protect your energy and strengthen yourself from the trauma we face. Don't willingly accept trauma just to find a way to deal with it. When I stated not to avoid confrontation it was confronting the need to forgive and forget. When trauma occurs, you cannot avoid it now, so take care of yourself. Once you're in it there's no escape so deal with it. We're humans at the end of every day which means when we're hurt it's hard to forgive or forget those moments.

As unfortunate as life tends to be there's a need for a solution, an easier way to bridge the gap between trauma and forgiving yourself. That's the common denominator between the two. YOU. Start by analyzing you. What did you do? What can you do? Question your motives. Figure out your desires. Your emotions play a vital role when dealing with trauma. Once we're hurt no matter if it's on the surface or a deep scar, emotionally; it's hard to forgive. Once you've searched your soul, the closer you should migrate to forgiveness. The situation isn't in your control; but you can control yourself in the situation. Whereas, by taking those steps you're trusting yourself to understand your situation. Building a solid trust with yourself bridges the gap between forgiving and forgetting. These things are considered a domino effect. You become traumatized, seek out forgiveness and take the time to forget about it. Trauma doesn't take a vacation from the mind. Once you've understood your situation completely is when you fill your mind with flooding thoughts. Think of how that situation changed you. Think of how that experience turned you into a stronger person. Think of how much you learned about love after your last heartbreak. We as humans get so caught up on the emotion, we neglect the enlightenment. It's no longer trauma but an experience now. It's no longer pain but now a journey. Forgiveness isn't for the weak but the strongest learn to forget. These tools are better used internally and over a period. Not in a moment but in whatever time it takes you to go through the motions. We hurt ourselves the most by rushing our healing from traumatic experiences. As much as it hurts to experience trauma it's that much more painful if not worse to heal. Especially alone. Therefore, if you have someone by your side take the time to appreciate them. Instead of battling with yourself you battled your trauma together. That's what I call bliss.

Forgiveness is what God breathes. Therefore, it's not an expectation for humans to forget rapidly. These things take time. Sometimes it takes years. Without the proper guidance it could take a lifetime but I'm here to guide you in the right direction. Life is an emotional roller coaster that leaves you questioning everything and everyone in it. It turns you away from love. It turns you towards drugs. It makes you cry. It leaves you up all night. Believe me, life can be hell. No matter how damaging life becomes, with the power to forgive and forget; you can outgrow the trauma that comes with living. Just as a flower withstands various storms and still blooms, is the same way you can grow beyond hurt. Remain diligent in your journey; success comes to those who are patient and steadfast. It'll all be worth it in the end.

GROWING PAINS

f you made it all the way to the end; use a semicolon. The metaphor is simple. By placing a period, you can end your pain, suffering, and sentences. Meanwhile, using a semicolon lets everyone know you have more to say. If you allowed God to have his way and work through you, it's not over. If you took all that pain on the chin; fighting tears, unsure you could continue, it's not over. Once you're willing and able to move beyond the pain placed by someone else it becomes about the pain you've caused yourself. The pain of growing could be just as bad if not worse than the pain of losing. Remember this, you can bear it my loved ones, trust me. You aren't a failure; you've succeeded in love. The complexities that surround love followed by its brokenness within a relationship may be something you lost out on, but you've gained an indecipherable amount of knowledge, in love, in life, through God, with wisdom. As complicated as it may seem, to grow one must hurt. Pain is inevitable, it's going to have weight on your life, but you will persevere. Growth within pain creates wisdom through struggle.

I won't sugarcoat the situation because whatever you place on a wound will still sting, so it might as well be painful at first and sweet in the end. Life is complicated. It'll take the sweetest thing and turn it sour. For example, you loved someone so much, you gave them not only your heart, but your mind, your body, even your soul and in the end, they spat in your face and left you broken. The hardest thing to comprehend is that holding onto something so tight; causes more pain than to let it go. No matter what you say, it's easier to let those kinds of situations go. Learn to let them go. We must grow, because holding onto the thoughts of what can be, will ruin what you will be. Learn from the love that you give out so effortlessly but receive so sporadically. Tell me how dark your past was, and I'll tell you how light your future can be. We occasionally get stuck in what could be instead of seeing what is. Considerably, we're all Kings and Queens but when we allow others to shed darkness on our light, we then fail ourselves. Love didn't do you wrong, God didn't fail you, and that person didn't destroy you. The reality of it all is that you stopped growing. You stopped thinking as an individual and loving as one whole. When you're in a relationship you are part of one whole, but your mind is still yours. Understand what your mind can take, what will break your spirits, what will fuel your soul, and what'll break your heart. People say you can't grow in a relationship and to me that's false, how else will you teach yourself in retrospect to another soul? How can you ever understand yourself as part of one whole? What I tend to notice often is how people are so selfish, they'd rather spend years figuring themselves out but give up within the first year of figuring someone else out. Me personally, I treat my relationships standardly, it's a give and take, never take more than you'll give and in many other instances never give more than you can take. You'll always fail if you love conditionally, whereas morally you'll always succeed loving unconditionally. When you say you love someone and want to be with someone that's the ultimate commitment, until you get married. That time between the first date and the proposal you're supposed to be committed. Then not only that you're supposed to learn yourself as an individual; learn your loved one as an individual, learn your loved one in consideration of yourself. Seemingly the process in a relationship is that you're forever learning but once you stop, then you'll end up complicating your growth process.

The process for growth can be put into a simple equation, G=L+U*T. To place that in words, Growth equals Learning plus Understanding multiplied by Time. As, time increases and progresses you then learn and gain various understanding which then equates to growth. The acronym is Glut, which is the root word of gluttony, to me interprets a lot. It's hard to grasp all those things but then again some of those that do have a sense of greed behind it because they've learned and now, they'll use that growth for negativity. If that becomes the case, then those who assume growth may have never grown. Never use growth for negative things because you will grow negatively to a degree that you won't comprehend down the line. I was and still am someone's child, but I've paid close attention to those around me for years and I tend to see it every so often, there's people who grow and use that growth to fuel negative outcomes. For example, the thing that fueled their heart might've been lust, they found love and then became broken hearted, but then proceeded to find God to overcome the painful situation but that didn't draw them closer to the Lord. This fueled their negative tendencies, which led them to follow temptation. I'm not stereotyping or assuming; these are just things I've seen in my daily life. Now not only do they have the power and wisdom of the lord, situational understanding, spiritual knowledge, as well as a free spirit from the negativity that could've ate them alive. Those people now can use all of this to manipulate and confuse those around them. That's something we all must be aware of, sheep in wolves clothing.

Growth can be complicated, it's a road without a map. A street with no end. Which in terms mean it's forever and ongoing; with no end, growth is a continuing process. Growth is what you make it, never let anyone define what your growth may be. It could be something as small as you not showcasing your anger or emotions negatively anymore. Which in your reality is a huge success because at a point in time you never thought you'd see the day. That's growth. Now, I'm not saying that if someone breaks your heart, move on and grow from it because it's never that simple, but it's a problem in which you need to progress in growth to learn and understand for the betterment of yourself. Which will happen in due time, but it's a never-ending process. The most complicated things require the most growth, it requires the most work. For example, you may not understand death or even want to accept it. That requires you to grow. Your mind is the strongest weapon in your arsenal, you'll become a zombie in this world without growth. Ask yourself would you rather grow and have unnatural pain from growth or just harbor pain from each person? Would you fight for your own harmony or live daily and being fruitful? Life will throw so many things at you that will drive those questions into our minds, and it'll continue to be our duty to successfully comprehend the answers to the questions and why. We must learn as counterparts to a whole success story, how to stand up within our own troubles. So many of us rather overstep our troubles, deny the fact of even having them, it'll even get to the point of confusing denial. You turn into someone without comprehension of success. It's not for me to tell you how to operate or continue to live but to inform you of the realities of life; we all tend to battle with some of the same things. Find the time to devote personally to yourself and seek out success within the rest, the silence, also various activities. Find ways around troubled topics. Find pathways to your own situational understandings but don't just lean onto your own understanding, lean on the teachers before us for guidance. For some that'll be God, study the bible, read to comprehend the scriptures pertaining to your situations, even constant conversation, as well as a constant need for his guidance. Spend the free time you must comprehend understandings of your situations, then lean on the understanding of the father above. For those that don't seek out God, seek wisdom. Philosophers, Astronomers, Consultants, including Therapists or psychiatrists. These are all people with wisdom, a method of higher learning. They seek achievement through knowledge not based of faith or religion. The proven facts of life. Statistics are the things that stand and not a living word compiled by many men about a specific being. It is not bashing the bible but explaining it in a more logical sense for those who do not understand spiritual terms so profusely. Once you can gain situational wisdom, enlightenment, then understandings beyond your own capacity, there must be action taken to push the success story into a reality. It takes work, diligence, and passion towards your own success to achieve the level of greatness that is assumed to be "the top of the reef." It begins within oneself. Once you search within, you'll then find out who you truly are; what you're truly capable of, what is passion to you, how passion is showcased, how your situations shaped you, honestly, there's so much you'll find and gain knowledge of. You fall but don't force yourself back up to recreate the same cycle. Don't fail to ignore the reasons you even felt defeated in the first place. So many of us find routines no matter what kind of failures come, stick to the routine and success will come. The reason I will not agree is because if you are focused on the same thing expecting a different outcome, you are insane. Insanity does not equate towards growth, insanity does not equate to peace, insanity does not complete your life in full unison. It is a constant failure that one becomes content with; hopefully to roll or fall into success. I'm driving you to go out and get it. No need to wait like chicken little for the piece of the sky to fall into your lap, take the pieces that you have and create a trail of breadcrumbs. Just in case things go wrong, you can then find your way back to success with the help from yourself, which can the progress into something else. This is one of the most complicated ways but in my opinion the most successful. Gain understanding. Don't let the complications make you fret, if success was easy then success rates would be higher than divorce rates, and divorce isn't easy at all. Success does not come out of the fallen sky, you might see that happen occasionally, you might also have those who have linear success which runs out faster than most like to acknowledge, but the exponential growth is more useful. You grow from the inside out, so now not only has your faith, wisdom, and comprehension as an adult or one seeking growth, grown, but you've patiently gained knowledge. From the inside out you've strengthened and healed parts of yourself that most shut off from the world, drink away, or suppress it in unhealthy manners rather than facing it. You've caressed and exposed success to your mind and it thrives of the thought, if backed by action. Everything about oneself will extended further than any understandings that one could have. In other words, your success depends on how much work you're willing to put forth for yourself. Your successes depend on the way you weather the various storms that life is so used to creating or recreating. Only you know what you can and won't take. Don't allow anyone to force change upon you; accept it to recognize the options and choices you must successfully choose from, then keep growing no matter how painful it may be.

Growing with pain creates a person prepared for the trials from the storms to showcase who can create pathways to success. There's only so much that some could hold on to if any can hold on; keep fighting. There's no storm too dark to be weathered. Keep the fight and press on. The pains of growing sometimes can be physical, even every other aspect you just must keep the faith through the temporary situational weeping momentums. Find peace within the tears and the pain because there's light at the end of every dark tunnel. You must keep the remembrance of the success within the situations. Your life will be complete with; hopes, dreams, aspirations, and happiness. It takes work. Never give up or give in no matter how much pain you endure before you try to grow or the pain that's endured during and or after the growth. Fight to control the sails through the stormy seas full of metaphoric sea monsters or natural disasters. You must learn how to stand firmly through adversity if success is what your goal in life is. The robotic routine life is made for many, some, like me must find success within another system, which is more complicated. As I stated before, the success within sets me apart from many so I'll choose the route that causes more pain; more storms, more hell, and even more vicious battles because they came from within. My darkness and or demons will be dealt with accordingly, which sets up my future or pathway to success. Growing pains aren't to run you away, or to make you cower, but to strengthen your being into something more complex and indestructible. Never stop growing, learning, and seeking wisdom. Progress to success comes with storms, just weather them.

HOW TO LOVE

Love is such an invigorating action that it transforms you into someone else. The moment you choose love it begins to consume your entire being. This feast turns you into someone more understanding. A person with more clarity. Love makes your soul smile. It causes you to spin on a merry-go-round and stare into the sky, amazed. The feelings can become confusing because of its various highs and lows. There are times love will hurt more than it heals, but that's okay. There will always be a lesson in the middle of pain.

We make love out to be the menace when it's the healing that scares us all. That inevitable moment in time where we learn that we've been too comfortable. It comes with a sigh of disparity, but an open mind filled with clarity. Love forces us all to heal. Self-love or even that of a relationship. The trauma we all know is almost hereditary. It's passed down through generations and still felt years later. Changing the love, we know of today. These weights we carry are the scars we never healed. These are the wounds we didn't allow the time to heal. The scabs we pick leave marks. When we don't heal, we're left in this world looking for love in all the wrong places. Love was never bad. Our intentions for love were bad and it worsened over time. We learn, it's a lot easier to stay in love once you fall. The complications come with self. As you continue to fall in love, can you still love yourself? Those healing pains hurt but what hurts worse is losing out on love because you aren't healed. Healing by yourself or in your relationship is STILL healing. We often let the words of others dictate our actions. When in love you realize that we have a choice. I can heal myself by doing these things for myself. I can grow with my person by doing these things. In both instances I am growing. That's the point of anything you do, growth.

Life without growth and development leaves dull unfinished products. As humans we happen to become zombified, begging for love to heal us once again. Love isn't a cure to the sorrow your spirit has faced. Love isn't a pastime that you can use to forget the crowded thoughts. Love is a punctuation mark. It's loud and disrespectful like your child who never listens. Love is complex in texture because the lessons aren't lyrics to a song. Love won't hug you some nights, that's just love. Having the common goal to grow leads to a level of love you never knew existed. It's important to heal all the quiet thoughts.

Sometimes setbacks are inevitable, and we happen to digress. That's okay too. Love doesn't require us to have it all together. She grants us the time to open our own minds and grind our own gears. It's the most eradicating experience but you learn about life. That time spent developing self is for the goodwill of your relationships. Afterwards you become a better aunt. A more attentive brother. Love heals those wounds by forcing the person to do the necessary inner work. Once we learn to fill our voids with healthier things, we will then begin to understand the true meaning of love. A fact that withstands all aspects of love, it's a choice. Therefore, no matter how much life sets you back. It's your choice to get up.

Love doesn't allow man to feel pity for himself. Love doesn't allow a woman to forget her children. These types of things are natural. Uncontrollable amounts of love that we give as humans. Then there's the emotion-based love. The love that is only fueled by the ways you make them feel. This love makes a man take care of a woman. This love makes a woman stay. Then you have the love that you choose.

That love you have for that aunt that annoys you. That love that you have with your abusive parents. That love is something you can't deny. The trauma that's attached to that love goes back to the world being created. It's the same love God had for the world or Jesus had for us as human. That love is unconditional, meaning that it will choose you no matter the circumstances. That's what I consider the love we should have for ourselves and the one we say we want to be with forever. That kind of love is what the movies referenced so beautifully. It requires sacrifice. Unconditional love isn't only written in the bible, it's what makes the world go round. All three are necessary in terms of being a good-hearted person. Natural love happens without your regard, but the emotion-based love is necessary for keeping the love fresh. Random gifts. Random texts. Activities. Dinner dates. These types of things make you feel love and remind you of what your heart feels. Unconditional love is necessary because it proves the vows that were told. Unconditional love means that at my worst you'll still hold my heart in reverence. Those three types of love are the *Eccentric Adulations*. Don't allow love to dictate your life, dictate how you'll live in love. Ask yourself how will you blossom as a flower amid the storms?

Truthfully, love is an unconditional choice. That choice can make you hate everything there is to understand about love. The reality of love is that somewhere along the way, life ruined you. That love you think you have in your mind, is the love that's missing in your heart. Once we come to that realization, we often take it straight to those we love the most. Those that unconditionally love you, will love you through it. They might make you cry or hurt you in ways you didn't expect but they will still love you. Then we can start to look within and analyze what's missing in ourselves, which complicates everything. As we venture into our spirits and finally hit the nails on the coffin, we realize where we went wrong. We begin the analysis of life. Learning more about ourselves in retrospect to someone else. We then learn that what we thought we did out of love, we did out of traumatic memory. What we assumed was their way of loving us, was their way of loving themselves. As a result, we were met with minimal amounts of love. Sometimes people don't love you. That's life. Love was never supposed to be this complicated we as people made it this way. Love is supposed to be unconditional. Without bound. I'm afraid we forget that we aren't full enough to become whole with someone else. Let this be a lesson to all that seek love and wisdom. Love yourself and learn to accept the love from someone else.

EPILOUGE

This message was inspired by growth... a mortal rose growing from the concrete jungles that surrounds him. Whenever it comes to loving yourself or loving someone else, continuous growth becomes the relationships requirement. As a result, one must take the pain in their hearts and accept it in their minds. Whether or not you can change the pain solely comes from within, so; when you find the answers you look for, GROW!

People misunderstand what love really brings to everyone. A heart full of love can learn the ways to master self. A mind full of love can recite vows that are meant to stand forever. A body that feels love can walk confidently with a head held high to the sky. See, love is not a fictional miracle that absorbs people. It is a spiritual connection to something everlasting. That is what amazes me about love. We all deal with so many things that life bring and some of you have lost love. Lost touch with passion. My hope for my readers is that this book brought you back to the center of your life. Realizing what we are all individually worth. This story started off a bit hazy, adding to the confusion on what love meant. After diving deep into our understandings, we looked at personal opinions; verbal statements, even cognitive progressions to decipher loves definition. What made love hard to define? Once we widened our perspective, we noticed that love too has a dark side, but also a spiritual as well as subconscious side. This makes defining something so simple, really complicated. Throughout the story I aimed to lead my readers through a metaphorical relationship between a hyper sense of self. Seeking the other side of your own thoughts and ideas. Looking through the lens to see the biggest picture that was so hard to see. The image that displays love as a choice that we should admire.

Learning that love was a choice could seem surreal in the beginning but after careful consideration. How else does someone find enjoyment after 26 years? What about the first few encounters? How do you know that you can trust someone you just met? This choice to live with love allows the individual the strength of being. The complications come when others lack that same love. Problems arises when someone give their all and nothing comes back in return. A conditional love leaves all hearts miserable. Seeking out the balance in a healthy unconditional love requires more than patience. The requirement sets the tone for the relationship whether it's personal or otherworldly. The main goal should be to love without a sheer doubt. Love without the fear of losing out because what is for you will remain beside you. Unconditional love is the potion that creates a dependency to be desired in any way from anyone. It heals the wounds we all find amid the trauma. I hope my readers learned the lesson that was on display; the picture we painted. Love is the unconditional choice that we all should make when considering ourselves or someone we'd like to date. Choose love.

AFTERWORD

One day back when I first went to college, I had a very hard time. I was alone in another state for the first time and that's typical, its college; but the difference was that I wasn't ready. I had a mental breakdown a few months prior with some loved ones, tearing up about becoming an adult. My fears as a young man becoming a grown man. I was concerned with my doubts and worries that lingered from the trauma I've faced. I was an emotional wreck that was shipped off to school. That emotional wreck turned into the titanic after freshman year. Along the way, I learned a lot more about myself. I guess you can say it was the first time I was aware of my growth.

This story however stems deeply but starting from that point forward, I learned how to love myself. Coming from a suicidal depressive state of mind. Where I was talking to the voices in my head and contemplating my death at least once a week. I learned how to love the skin I was in and forgive myself. I learned to cope and heal. I acquired a skill that sticks with me today; breathing. I learned how to control myself and regulate the chaos that stirs within me emotionally. As a black man the rage and anger are deeply rooted and fueled with passion and pain really. Therefore, I turned my weaknesses into my strengths and started to want love in the real form. That was when I met the newfound love of my life. I found someone I could grow for. Heal for. Achieve for. I cleaned myself up with her in mind. I spoke my truths and never told a lie again. I sought out religion and something to follow for spiritual guidance. I began healing old wounds and afterwhile she was all I did this for.

That was until I started to look inward. I wrote this book thinking of the powers that love be. After loving myself I learned how to love someone else, and this book became a miracle made. As I developed as a boyfriend and grew alongside my girlfriends I started to realized what was actually at stake here. Love is such a dynamic force that persuades the individual to become better.

I started with three chapters. The first three with an idea to generally read the book from front cover to back and vice versa with a different message being told. That way you started based upon your status in love. Instead, I held onto those same three chapters for about a year. For a year I could grasp the concept of what I truly aimed to do here. I wanted this to be more than a cliché love story. I wanted this to fuel others to comprehend how to love yourself better as well as someone else. What I did next came from an equation in my mind. If I want this book to feel real or hit hard I need to speak on specific topics. I already got the introductory hook in chapter one and the story in chapter three but how could I move forward? I thought about it. If I want my readers to heal and grow, then they must read what healing and growth sounds like. Then the chapters came to me individually. I started with I need you and each chapter after had this simple equation. Write how you feel about needing someone in your notes. Then in the document write out what you think about those very same feelings. The book had been separately written out probably the second or third year of me starting but these final two had specific requirements. I took those thoughts and feelings then edited those ideas to convolve into a true understanding of something so confusing. The trail of tears is the journey through to self-healing. I wrote a guide on love. A guide that weighs in on the negative but explains the positive. The element of growth in love was written for all to heal. Heal and prepare for the second coming of the trilogy that involves life. We solved love but now its time to live and learn about life. In the meantime, I hope each individual reader took the time to look inward to heal yourself.

ABOUT THE AUTHOR

For me, growing up was harder than it should've been. The love around me was very limited, but it started to swell up over time. I personally feel deeply for any and everything. I am a bit sensitive. My only problem was that the world taught me how to be cold and callous. Therefore, the journey of this young man's life began in 1999 on a summer night at the beginning of June. I was born to lead; I can recall times where my mom reiterating the fact that she didn't give birth to a follower. No matter what, she wanted me to be my very best self, every day. Those times when I wasn't my best, she made sure I was reminded of her disappointments. I grew to recognize the strength that discipline wielded, even though it took about 19 years. I learned quite a bit along this lifetime and its not to say I know more than the next person because I too lack knowledge in a lot of things. However, I am quite intelligent. I use my intelligence to my advantage; like this for example. This book I wrote was something that I truly developed my whole life. Not only did I learn what love meant, but also what it meant to me. As an adolescent I learned the power of my words. I learned the weight of my decisions and although I didn't always make the right ones, I learned quite a bit through the processes of trial and error. Every error left me standing trial until the point I was faced with a real trial and jury. From that moment forward I reflected on every decision, every encounter, even every part of me that felt incomplete. I handed it over to God and kept working at the things that went unseen. I kept working to develop a better version of me. It started with loving unconditionally, and that's where it will end with me. I strive to be the absolute best product of God that he intended me to become. My only prayer is that everyone else does the same.